The Spokesman
The Kurdish Question in Turkey

Edited by Tony S[...]

Published by Spokesm[...]
Bertrand Russell Peace [...]
Ken Coates: Editor 1[...]

[...]okesman 119

Subscriptions
Institutions £38.00
Individuals £20.00 (UK)
£25.00 (ex UK)

online
[...]s available

[...]logue record
[...]k is available
[...] the British Library

CONTENTS

Thanks To Steve Bell

*Cover: Waiting outside Silivri Court, next to
Europe's largest prison campus, 60 km from Istanbul.*

Published by the
Bertrand Russell Peace
Foundation Ltd.,
Russell House
Bulwell Lane
Nottingham NG6 0BT
England
Tel. 0115 9784504
email:
elfeuro@compuserve.com
www.spokesmanbooks.com
www.russfound.org

FSC
Mixed Sources
Product group from well-managed
forests and other controlled sources

Cert no. SGS-COC-006541
www.fsc.org
© 1996 Forest Stewardship Council

Editorial

The Kurdish Question in Turkey

Ayse Berktay has been locked up in a Turkish prison since October 2011. Her home in Istanbul was raided in the early morning, as she described in *Spokesman 115*:

> 'I was taken into custody at 5am on 3 October 2011, when my house was raided by the police. All of us were taken into custody in the same way, at approximately the same hour. My door was not broken down, but the doors of some were. Some of our friends, not at home when the police arrived, went to Party Headquarters (BDP – Peace and Democracy Party) to find out what was going on and what could be done, and were then taken into custody themselves from there … '

She and some 200 others are, periodically, before Turkey's Tribunal with Special Powers as part of the 'KCK trials'. KCK stands for Kurdish Communities Union, which the Turkish government has labelled a 'terrorist' organisation, although the actual basis for this draconian claim is not at all clear.

In 2009, the Turkish government under Prime Minister Erdogan launched a massive campaign of repression against the KCK and BDP memberships. As the BDP gained more electoral successes, so the repression increased. In the 2009 elections, the BDP doubled the number of towns and cities it administers, gaining more than 80 per cent of the vote in some places. It has an overwhelming majority in Diyarbakir, the largest city in Turkey's Kurdish areas in the south-east. In June 2011, defying repression, the Party had 36 representatives elected to Turkey's Parliament, comfortably passing the excessively high threshold of 10 per cent of the vote to gain entry.

The situation worsened that year, when secret talks ceased between the Turkish intelligence services and representatives of Abdullah Öcalan, the imprisoned Kurdish leader. Since then, there have been more waves of arrests of Kurdish political activists and their Turkish comrades, including Ayse. These continue. Some ten thousand people have been imprisoned, often in pre-trial detention, which can last up to ten years in Turkey. Such protracted detention is contrary to all civilised norms, and has been the subject of persistent complaint and criticism by the Council of Europe and the European Union.

In December 2012, many Kurds, some Turks and various others gathered at the European Parliament in Brussels to consider 'The Kurdish Question in

Activists in Turkey led away under arrest

New pipeline through Kurdish areas of Turkey?

'... Stretching for miles under a ridge of brown, rugged hills near the Turkish border, Shaikan is huge ... Oil finds such as Shaikan have made Kurdistan, an autonomous region in the north of Iraq, one of the biggest draws in the global oil industry. It has attracted $10 billion in investment from foreign oil companies – a vast amount for a country of only 4.9 million people ... Initially, the region was the playground of wildcatters – small buccaneers with a big appetite for risk. But now the big boys are moving in. Over the past year, ExxonMobil, Chevron and Total have been grabbing some of the 45 billion barrels of oil thought to lie underneath Kurdistan.

... In 2008, there were only three drilling rigs in Kurdistan. This year there are 24 and next year there will be 40. Production, at about 200,000 barrels a day, will reach 250,000 b/d next year. By 2015, Kurdistan hopes to be exporting 1m b/d. To achieve this will require a major reconfiguration of the region's export infrastructure. The current Baghdad-controlled pipeline is plagued by bottlenecks. Many believe that Kurdistan will build its own pipeline into Turkey, giving it full control over exports. If this happens, the Kurdistan Regional Government will receive oil revenues directly from Turkey, rather than via Baghdad. This will give the KRG the economic independence many Kurds have long craved and build on the close relationship evolving between Kurdistan and its neighbour, Turkey ...'

Guy Chazan, 'An ocean of reserves waiting to be tapped'
Financial Times Special Report, 'Kurdistan Oil & Gas'
10 December 2012

Turkey'. The conference was sponsored by the United European Left/Nordic Green Left (GUE/NGL) political group, with support from Greens and Socialists. It had the sub-title, 'time to renew the dialogue and resume direct negotiations'. Notwithstanding attempts by the Turkish authorities to restrict Kurdish participation, the conference heard from many speakers of diverse backgrounds and nationalities. They included two prominent Kurds, Leyla Zana, now a member of the Turkish Parliament, who was previously imprisoned there, and Zübeyir Aydar of the KNK, who participated in the aborted negotiations with the Turkish intelligence services (the so-called 'Oslo Process') that ceased in 2011. We publish their papers here, alongside Ayse's own statement from prison on receiving an award from Turkish PEN, part of an international organisation which supports persecuted authors. Our Dossier section includes eyewitness accounts from some of the ongoing KCK trials.

Early in 2013, it seems that negotiations between the Turkish authorities and the Kurds may resume, once again. Might there be a constructive outcome this time? The day after the Turkish media reported that the Turkish government was discussing a 'road map' with Mr Öcalan, three Kurdish women activists were killed in Paris. They included Mr Öcalan's long-time comrade in the Kurdish Workers' Party (PKK), Sakine Cansiz. These 'executions, as they were described by the French authorities, seem calculated to undermine any 'road map' or other negotiations.

Some weeks earlier, Mr Öcalan had called for the end of hunger strikes amongst hundreds of Kurdish prisoners, which received an immediate and positive response from the strikers. These had threatened a major crisis in Turkey. As Leyla Zana reminds us, 'there can be a war without Öcalan, but there cannot be peace without Öcalan'. And there is already much war in the region, particularly in Syria. At the same time, the West wants to exploit Iraqi Kurdistan's massive oil reserves and export them through a new pipeline via the Kurdish areas of Turkey's south-east (see box). This may help to explain the somewhat more sympathetic hearing the Kurds are now receiving internationally.

Ayse Berktay

Unite Community Membership

find your **voice**

shape your **community**

- Take action in your local community
- Benefit from our offers and services
- Special discounted rate of 50p a week

If you are over 16 and not in paid work,
join us today. For more information, contact:

E: community@unitetheunion.org
W: www.unitetheunion.org

Len McCluskey
General Secretary

Tony Woodhouse
Chair, Unite Executive Council

www.unitetheunion.org/community

The arduous business of peace

Leyla Zana MP

The author is a member of the Turkish Parliament and recipient of the European Parliament's Sakharov Prize for Freedom of Thought. This article is based on her speech in Brussels in December 2012.

At this Kurdish conference organised in the European Parliament I am speaking in Turkish as a Kurd. This is because, as is the case in all institutional domains, the European Union cannot overcome the issue of Kurdish interpretation due to its approach which takes states rather than peoples as a basis. Thus, in order to be understood correctly, I need to speak in a language other than my mother tongue.

The global crisis the world is going through does not detract from the importance of the European Union as a peace project; on the contrary, it puts it in sharp relief. That the European Union provides support for peace initiatives undertaken in its neighbouring geographical areas also has to do with its vision of peace, which is shaped by European values. On the occasion of this conference, which is an effort to seek peace, I would like to congratulate the European Union for receiving the Nobel Peace Prize this year. The fact that the Nobel Peace Prize is given to Europe is testimony to the fact that the EU is a peace project as well as being an economic union. At a time when the Middle East is being reshaped, democracy, freedom and the yearning for peace, as values created by the European Union, continue to be crucial for humanity.

In 2012, poverty and inequalities in income distribution are on a global scale. Nuclear weapons, weapons of mass destruction, and policies giving priority to security shake the world. Therefore, continental Europe has to clarify its position *vis-à-vis* the rest of the world, and in relation to the Kurds in particular. The call for freedom of these people who live in the heart of the Middle East needs to be taken into consideration and supported by Europe.

Kurds, whose geography was fragmented one hundred years ago, are crossing a historic threshold today. In all the countries in which they live, they are raising the struggle for democracy, rights and freedoms. The Kurdistan Regional Government of Iraq is a guarantee not only for Kurds but also for the freedom and voluntary co-operation of all the ethnic and religious groups in that area. Western Kurdistan is a candidate for being a haven for all people escaping the wrath of the Baath Party and Assad. Kurds of Eastern Kurdistan continue to voice pleas for freedom while taking the risk of being executed by the Iranian regime. The Kurds of Northern Kurdistan, on the other hand, influence the policies of Turkey and the Middle East as the most important element of Turkey's process of democratisation.

Finally, in 2012, Kurds demonstrated to the whole world that they are not a fragmented people living separately from each other. In all the countries in which they live, they are struggling not against people but against the cruel face and authoritarian character of those states.

The gains achieved during the last one hundred years in the Kurdish people's search for rights, justice and freedom, for which they gave their lives, are still coming under attack. The recent tensions between Iraqi Kurdistan and the central Iraqi government, where the central government has violated the constitution by which it is bound and has massed arms and troops in the Kurdish region, give rise to concerns. One cannot and must not remain silent in the face of a situation where people seeking democracy and stability could be drawn into a new conflict.

The fact that Syrian Kurds have not become a party to the crisis that country is in, that they have negotiated with patience and maturity, is an exemplary demonstration of responsibility that should be supported. Any attempts to block them from obtaining their rights, which entitlement stems from their status as a people, will constitute a far from just and fair solution.

Meanwhile, the gains achieved by Iranian Kurds are becoming lost amongst the undercurrents of the regime. For Iranian Kurds to institutionalise their gains they should, first and foremost, put into practice an *esprit de corps,* and those sensitive to their claims should speak up.

Turkey's trial with the Kurdish issue has not shaken that country's hundred-year-old cliché-ridden rhetoric. 'Improvements' in the Kurdish issue amount to no more than arrangements without an infrastructure; 'improvements' put in place with a mentality that says 'this is how I've done it; it's done!' Not only is there no constitutional or statutory initiative aimed at returning confiscated rights, but also the police and judiciary pressures on the Kurdish political movement are gradually increasing.

The report card of the Turkish state on the Kurdish issue during the last decade comprises cross border military operations; the statistics of our people who have been killed; the dialogue initiated with the Kurdistan Workers' Party (PKK) was not continued; the unlawful imprisonment of Mr Abdullah Öcalan goes on; military operations continue; arrests of politicians, with new ones being made day by day; the murder of Ceylan Önkol and dozens of children; the Roboski massacre has been covered up; and, lastly, the recent threat to remove the political immunity of Kurdish Members of Parliament. These are some of the serious obstacles to creating an environment of confidence.

Today, about ten thousand political detainees and convicted persons are held in Turkish prisons because they are active in the Kurdish political movement. These political detainees have, in recent months, risked their lives by subjecting their bodies to hunger for 68 days as the only remaining instrument in their hands to overcome the impasse in the Kurdish issue. As a result of national and international public opinion taking some ownership of the hunger strikes, channels of dialogue between the two parties were opened and, upon Mr Öcalan's call to the detainees, which was regarded as a positive initiative, the action was ended. A threshold, which could have swept the country into deep chaos in case of loss of life in the hunger strikes, was not crossed through wisdom and common sense. This is pleasing for the peace of country. Ending the hunger strike has placed on the agenda the achievement of a lasting peace. It has also increased hopes of solving the issue through dialogue and negotiations.

Peace is a very arduous business, and establishing an environment of confidence is the *sine qua non* of such a process.

That issues are actually being discussed is a positive development. However, words and rhetoric are no longer adequate in our society, and it is seen clearly that a process of moves two steps forward and one step back cannot heal any wounds at all.

In solving the Kurdish issue we need sincere and concrete steps focused on finding a solution. To this end, the government must, as soon as possible, put in place its concrete proposals for solving the Kurdish issue through dialogue and negotiations within the framework of a 'Peace Project' in which all parties' effective participation is ensured. In order not to delay this anymore, all friends of the Kurdish and Turkish people must joint their efforts for such a crucial project.

The human rights, political rights and basic freedoms of the Kurdish people that were seized must take their place in the new constitution. We do not want a new constitution that is 'just a new constitution no matter how it is', but one which includes all organs and foundations of the state. While solving the Kurdish issue, we are insistent on a democratic constitution that will check and limit the ruling party, and one that will prevent the state from being cruel to its citizens.

Take a look at the on-going debates in Turkey, which is on the brink of developing a new constitution. There is no talk of democratic initiatives that will open up the clogged system, that will help the people to breathe and that will solve chronic problems, first and foremost the Kurdish issue. With the existing 10 per cent electoral threshold, the political parties law and electoral law, proper democratic mechanisms are not even on the agenda.

The new constitution must guarantee peace and equality legislation for the peoples of Turkey. While Turkey tries to solve its chronic problems, it needs the European Union route and motivation. This is because the system in Turkey believes it needs to solve the Kurdish issue, but due to the character of the regime, it cannot develop an initiative for a solution as it cannot give up statism and nationalism. It is, therefore, trying to defer a solution to the problem, and trying to manage it to save the day. It simply cannot demonstrate its goal and its will to solve the issue.

Above all, if a future that includes Kurds is wanted, short, medium and long-term goals must be declared to the people and to the political institutions. Kurds should not be expected to forgo all their legitimate demands in return for a few palliative measures. Kurdish people should absolutely have political status in the 21st century. Otherwise, we may have to place on our agenda some actions in line with the 'Twin Conventions' signed by Turkey in 2003, which include the right to self-determination. Turkey has to move on to the concept of dialogue and negotiations instead of war and terrorism in relation to the Kurdish issue. To this end, we expect an open demonstration of political will that will transparently continue the interrupted Oslo Process, even though it may not be called the Oslo Process.

Politically motivated police and judiciary pressure targeting Kurdish politicians must end. A general amnesty that will open up the way for political solutions must be placed on the agenda. The initiative launched by the government under the names of the Kurdish Initiative or the Democratic Initiative must continue, with channels of dialogue to be established with the negotiating parties.

The state must refrain from making confusing strategic moves. There is no problem regarding negotiating partners and roles. It must be emphasised that, in solving the Kurdish issue, the general strategy must be negotiated with Mr Öcalan, the arms issue with the PKK, and constitutional and legislative arrangements with the Peace and Democracy Party (BDP) and all other Kurdish political circles. Efforts other than these simply lose time. Therefore, the state must develop an open solution strategy with the PKK, must open up the way for Mr Öcalan's effective participation in the process and demystify Imrali, where Mr Öcalan is kept in prison. It should be recognised that 'there can be a war without Öcalan, but there cannot be peace without Öcalan'.

We expect the European Union, which is founded on hundreds of years of experience, to take on a more active role in the process of solving Turkey's Kurdish issue. For Turkey, the Kurdish issue has completed its phase of finding recipes. The actors are clear and open. What's needed is to be realistic. The solution lies in the political institutions. Turkey cannot solve this issue by pressurising Kurdish politics and laying asphalt over it. Flowers cannot blossom in asphalt.

Time to talk

Zübeyir Aydar

*Mr Aydar was one of the
Kurds negotiating via the
Turkish intelligence
services in Oslo, until
talks broke down in 2011.
He is a member of the
Executive Board of the
Kurdistan National
Congress (KNK), and
spoke of his experience at
the Oslo negotiations to a
conference at the
European Parliament in
Brussels in December
2012. This was the ninth
International Conference
on the European Union,
Turkey and the Kurds,
organized by the EU
Turkey Civic Commission
and the United European
Left/Nordic Green Left
(GUE/NGL) political
group.*

I will try to express the Kurds' point of view on dialogue, negotiations, a road map, a political solution and peace. I will try to answer what Kurds understand by these concepts, what our approach is, have we done any work on them, and how we see the current situation.

Without going into the history, I will evaluate the last 34 years and will try to put forward a solution. Furthermore, I will speak in the context of the last Kurdish revolt, which has been developing under the leadership of the Kurdistan Workers' Party (PKK). Discussions on the solution to the Kurdish question began in the early 1990s with the efforts of the then President, Mr Turgut Ozal. The Kurdish side's response has always been positive; hence, on 17th March 1993, the PKK declared a unilateral ceasefire to search for solutions to pave the way. But, after the suspicious death of President Ozal, the response of the other party was not positive. Thus, this initiative failed and the cease-fire broke down.

In 1995 and 1998, similar initiatives took place and again, both times, the Kurdish side responded positively by declaring a unilateral cease-fire. However, the state's negative approach meant the attempts failed, as previously.

At the beginning of 1999, Mr Abdullah Öcalan was captured in Kenya as a result of an international conspiracy and handed over to Turkey, unlawfully. Despite this, the Kurds continued to search for solutions. After discussions with Mr Öcalan in prison, another cease-fire was declared in July 1999. Unlike other cease-fires, guerrilla forces had withdrawn beyond Turkey's borders in order to offer the least provocation. This situation continued until 2004. Unfortunately, the Turkish state and its actors took no further steps towards a solution during this time. When the conflict was suspended due to the cease-fire, the government said the problem was solved. On the other hand, Kurds shared many declarations with the public on how to solve the Kurdish question, such as road maps. These demands were extremely reasonable and acceptable, but they were ignored. The Kurds' well-intentioned calls were not heard; our behaviour seen, rather, as weakness.

Therefore, in June 2004, the conflict restarted. The government ignored it at first, but, from mid-2005 onwards, began again to discuss solutions. In 2006, the search for new solutions and initiatives became operational. The Kurds responded both times, when discussions began in 2005, and to the initiatives that took place in 2006, and accordingly declared cease-fires. To this day, including the first in 1993, the Kurds have declared eight cease-fires in total. All the cease-fires have broken down, due to the Turkish military's practice of abiding by the cease-fires very little or not at all, and the Turkish state's attitude in the face of deadlock.

The consultation process, and the developing dialogue of 2006 and its aftermath, should be separately assessed. At the beginning, this process was started indirectly by agencies who were delivering the messages. From the end of 2007, it developed into face-to-face consultations – known publicly as the Oslo Consultation. This consisted of two sides, one of whom was Mr Öcalan, who is in Imrali Prison, and the other being representatives of political organisations. These talks were carried out in parallel communication so as to support each other. The form of communication between the two sides was executed by exchange of written documents. Throughout this time, despite interruption and blocking, the process continued until July 2011. This process was prevented from reaching agreement because the government counterparty did not keep its pledges/promises, and did not try to resolve problems; instead, postponing arranged appointments.

Everyone can rightly ask: 'what has been discussed during this period, who has been talking, and why has there not been any significant progress?' The Kurdish side, who sought a political solution, approached the matter cordially and did their duty. In the first place, the most important step for the Kurds was a cease-fire. Apart from failed talks, it was only the Kurds from their side who declared a cease-fire, and complied with it – however, the Turkish military also, informally and partly, complied with the cease-fire process. The Kurds had no other agenda than resolving the political predicament with peace and dialogue, and all demands/claims were addressed. Those claims were very reasonable and logical; they wouldn't even need to be discussed under normal conditions of democracy. The road map for the resolution and protocols, including practical stages, were prepared and offered to the counterparts. The road map and claims were made public.

As regards the Turkish demands, with the purpose of being sincere about the peace deal and showing a non-violent way of solution (and also empowering the Turkish government in the peace process and dialogue), the Kurdish side sent back to Turkey a group of people consisting of guerrillas and people from the Maxmur Refugee Camp with a letter which included peaceful intentions. Although the counterparty promised not to arrest or try them, these people bringing the peace message were arrested and sentenced to heavy terms in prison.

Although the Turkish counterpart repeatedly made promises in this process, they never sat around the table with the peace group. They usually said 'we will discuss these points with our government and, at the next meeting, we will bring their response', but they never came back with a satisfactory answer. When the main subjects were discussed they claimed that they were not fully authorized. The Kurdish side proposed bringing a fully authorized committee in order to finalise the consultation, but the counterparty has not agreed on this subject at all.

While the consultations were becoming more frequent, the government was proposing a solution of the Kurdish predicament, a cease-fire was declared by the Kurds, which meant everyone; we were full of hope for a positive outcome. On 14 April 2009, the government's KCK operation against Kurdish politicians targeted even elected ones – we called this a 'political massacre'– and started a rush to arrest many people. When this matter was raised at the discussions, the counterparty's response was 'this is not our government's attitude, it is just some interfering prosecutors who carried out the operation and the arrested people will be at liberty, shortly'. Despite their promise, the arrests continue on a wide scale. Today, the number of arrested people continues to increase and has reached the tens of thousands.

At the beginning of 2011, the Turkish counterparty renewed the anti-Kurdish alliance with Iran, Iraq and Syria. According to their plan, based on the 'Sri Lanka-Tamil' model, those countries were to attack from all sides together, and aim to destroy the Kurdish Freedom Movement. In July 2011, this plan was put into action.

In face of all that has happened, the perception occurred on the Kurdish side that the Turkish side needed a cease-fire to conduct the elections in a comfortable environment, is in the process of gaining time through negotiation delays, and is working to make the final hit when they find the opportunity to do so. Actual practice validates this perception.

Today the negotiations have stopped. There have been heavy battles since July 2011. The Tamil-Sri-Lanka model, to which the AKP government has clung, did not work in Kurdistan. Once again, there are debates about the solution in Turkey. The answer will be positive to the question 'if there is a demand for new debates, how will the Kurdish side look at it?' However, we will look particularly for seriousness and sincerity; we have had enough of delays.

In Turkey, especially amongst those close to government, there are debates about the 'PKK is something else to the Kurdish quest', Imrali is different, Qendil is different, Europe is different', 'the organisation is the vendor of other powers'. These arguments are developed in the psychological war centres. They are made to muddy the issues and deepen the deadlock in the Kurdish question. Let's say this very clearly: without taking the movement that is fronted by the PKK into account, it is impossible to find a solution to the Kurdish question. There are no different views or heads in the organization; the organisation is a whole and its leader is Mr Abdullah Öcalan. The agenda of the organisation is the Kurdish question and Kurdistan; the welfare and freedom of the Kurdish people. There are no other agendas apart from this; in particular, it has no act or aim that will serve foreign powers.

On the question of foreign powers, we need to touch especially on the attitude of European and western powers. The attitude of the West to date has not been to serve the cause of solution; on the contrary, its attitude is to support those who are against the solution. All those with a conscience will know that the struggle for freedom of the Kurdish people is a just and legitimate movement. Accusing this struggle of terrorism is an injustice; lawlessness is on the side of cruelty. The West accuses the Kurdistan freedom struggle of terrorism and inclines against Kurdish politicians and institutions while providing arms and support to Turkey. It is obvious that this attitude deepens the deadlock. It is not possible to reach a solution without removing the terror listing and the actions that are carried out on that basis.

Our attitude on the Kurdish side is open and clear. Our demands are a minimum that should happen in a democratic country. The suggestions that I will present now, even if they are not the same word for word, are those that we have provided to the other side and the public on many different occasions. In this framework, I would like, once again, to present our proposals for a solution.

1) Representatives of all people with a different background should

participate during the preparation of the new constitution in order for it to be democratic. On this basis, the new constitution should either be based on constitutional citizenship and be neutral to all ethnic identities, or Kurdish identity should be recognized and take its place in the constitution.

2) With recognition of Kurdish identity, the Kurdish language is to be regulated in education and used from primary school to university. The Kurdish language to be recognized as a second official language in the heavily Kurdish-populated areas.

3) Removal of all obstacles to survival and development of Kurdish culture, and all the rights afforded to other cultures to be recognized for Kurdish culture. There must be no restrictions on TV, radio or press.

4) Freedom of thought, belief, expression and association by removing barriers to free politics.

5) Introduction of a Democratic Local Government Act. Democratic local authorities, including local councils, particularly by increasing the on-site management approach to ensure democratic autonomy.

6) Abolition of the village guard system based on economic and social measures.

7) Social wounds must be dressed and healed in order to restore crippled social balances to a healthy state again by removing all obstacles that obstruct those who were forced to leave their villages and encourage their return. Damages incurred by war victims must be met. In addition, administrative, legal and financial support must be made available to the villagers so that they can rebuild their villages.

8) Commitment to launch in the Kurdish areas a campaign of economic development and government-backed investments. Private sector investment, mainly in the form of cheap credit, tax cuts and incentives should be provided from other sources.

9) Social peace and democratic participation of Kurdish and Turkish communities on the basis of the enactment of law should pardon one another mutually. Everyone, including all political prisoners, and Mr. Abdullah Öcalan, should be free to join in social and political life. Political refugees living abroad should also be included in democratic political life.

10) Together with the provision of a permanent solution within the framework of existing laws, guerrillas or the local police force to protect the new arrangements in the presence of a democratic status.

Practical tasks are:

1) The two sides, including representatives of political parties and non-

governmental organizations and the establishment of a Constitutional Council, which will discuss the constitutional and legal issues.

2) Representatives of the two sides and the relevant powers, and the establishment of a Peace Council that will address issues regarding security and the armed forces.

3) In order to ensure confidence in the democratic peace and reconciliation process, a Research and Justice Commission must be established to investigate and reveal truths about any human right violations that have been committed.

4) Through these councils and commissions direct communication with Mr. Abdullah Öcalan must be ensured.

The position of Mr. Abdullah Öcalan needs to be clarified. Mr. Öcalan is the leader and founder of the movement, and has the legal right to veto decisions. At the same time, he is the only person with wide authority throughout the overall organization, the armed forces, and the youth structure, as well as the people. He is the chief negotiator for the Kurdish side. In order for the negotiations to be productive, his free movement, as well as his health and safety, must be ensured.

In our opinion, all these things are possible. These are our suggestions. We are ready to listen, evaluate and consider all suggestions made by others.

Questioning 'terror'

Ayse Berktay

Ayse Berktay has been in prison since October 2011. She is one of thousands, as she explains (see Spokesman 115, also). Her trial, with some 200 other activists in the Peace and Democracy Party (the BDP) has been adjourned again, until March 2013. As a celebrated writer and translator, Ayse's case has been taken up by PEN International, which has long campaigned in support of persecuted authors. In that connection, she recently received an award in memory of Duygu Asena, herself an acclaimed Turkish journalist, author and activist for women's rights, who died in 2006.

It is with love and affection that I remember Duygu Asena, on this occasion which is held in her honour, and I send my own greetings and love to you from Bakirköy Prison. I very much wish I could be with you in person, looking at your faces and into your eyes as I speak and listen. For I am of the opinion that these times require tremendous effort on our part if we are to clearly express our thoughts and feelings and the stance we take, and to sincerely explain ourselves and genuinely understand the person sitting across from us. In my case, the communication will have to be one-sided, and for that I apologize. It is always possible for you to overcome this one-sidedness and to give me the chance to listen, too; I would be more than happy to do so.

First, I must thank you for this meaningful award. Duygu Asena was a woman who bravely defended her beliefs, who spoke out candidly about her priorities, who lived what she believed, and never backed down in her struggle to break certain taboos. She was a feminist who advocated women's right to 'be' themselves, for human rights, and for the right to freedom of thought and expression. I view this award as a meaningful act of defiance in the face of the injustice and audacious disregard for the law that has resulted in the imprisonment of myself along with over 200 fellow members of the Peace and Democracy Party (BDP), 34 of whom are women. The case brought against us forms part of a continuing mass political hunt which completely disregards the freedom to practise politics, the freedoms of thought and speech, and the freedom to organize. All this constricts democratic political space and, by targeting the BDP, aims to render the Party ineffective, disempowering the people who support it. This is not a case of a few 'innocents' who happened to get mixed up with a gang of criminals; it is, through and through, a massacre of law, democracy, and freedom.

According to the indictment, the Platform of Peace Initiatives, which consists of various smaller peace initiatives started by artists, women, anti-war activists, conscientious objectors, anti-militarists, and intellectuals, is a 'subsidiary organ of a terrorist organization'; so, too, is the Democratic City Council established by dozens of parties, political journal publishers and their followers, legal chambers, non-governmental organizations, environmental and urban movements, unions, organisations, grassroots movements, and neighbourhood and identity-based movements. This trial is based upon an indictment that claims peace is something that can only be arrived at by two states. According to the same indictment, the belief that the state should engage in peace talks with the Kurdistan Workers' Party (PKK) and Abdullah Öcalan, or even 'maintaining that the PKK is not a terror organization', is evidence of PKK membership. According to this indictment, reading, conducting research, or trying to come up with different proposals for ways to end the conflict are evidence that one is a member of the PKK. Efforts to secure the release of terminally ill prisoners, writing letters to prisoners, and visiting prisoners are evidence of PKK membership. Efforts to ensure women's participation in politics and to make sure they have a say in party decisions are a crime. Citing the injustice of court verdicts, wanting military operations to stop, and mourning the dead are all crimes. People are deemed guilty of belonging to the PKK, based on their thoughts and the words and concepts that they use. The 2,401-page indictment is full of hundreds of examples showing this to be the case.

In the indictment, it is blatantly proclaimed that insistence upon the right to defend oneself in the mother tongue does not derive from any human necessity, and this position has been affirmed by the courts. The culmination of refusing to recognize this right is the refusal to allow even those friends of ours with whom we have difficulty communicating in Turkish to have an interpreter present in court for their testimony. In the courtroom, the defendant will, of course, speak in the language in which he or she best expresses him or herself; this is a matter of the very livelihood of the defendant. And who knows better than the defendant which language he or she understands best? There is only one explanation for the denial of this very basic reality, the refusal to recognize this very basic right, and the misery that so many people are made to endure in the prisons as a consequence: language is being used as a means to dominate and tyrannize.

We are people engaged in the world of writing and poetry; we live, eat, and breathe language. We could write books about the importance of language in a person's life, the sources from which each language feeds, how it develops, the death of languages and the reasons therefore, and what it means for posterity. Only we ourselves know the torment we each endure in our quest to find the best words to express a feeling, a thought, a dream delivered on the wings of a bird, a scent, hope and desperation, love and pain. Only we know how to draw that information, those intuitions, and to what depths of our souls and stories and memories of our childhood we must plunge to retrieve them. That much we should know.

Only a person whose mother tongue has been banned can know just how vital her connection with the mother tongue is. Only she can feel this in her heart; only she, and we. We know, most of all, that to ban education in the mother tongue and its use in public space, that is, constricting the space in which the language functions, means the obliteration of a people, an identity and a culture, and the murder of a language. We can make it possible for those who do not suffer this plight to understand and to feel what it means. One must realize that such a fundamental injustice is nothing less than dynamite placed beneath the foundation of peace and harmony.

We know that languages are the memories of nature and humanity, and that obliterating a language is a crime, a crime against humanity, which means obliterating a piece of the family of humanity, a crime which cannot be undone. Whether we realize it or not, we possess the knowledge that the pain and victimization of a people or peoples whose memories are under attack and in danger of being erased, render us all victims, that the voices which are lost mean our own impoverishment as well. And all of this knowledge brings with it responsibility: the responsibility to take steps rendered necessary by such knowledge.

This state of affairs begs a question: how to explain the fact that we who are so closely engaged with language, have failed to stand up and join our voices with those who have been demanding education in the [Kurdish] mother tongue for ten years, and the right to defend oneself in court in the mother tongue for three-and-a-half years?

I'm looking at our court case, a travesty of justice, democracy, and freedom, at the increasingly commonplace infringements against human rights, and how those infringements are rendered somehow 'legitimate', at how the massacres in Antep and Afyon are made to disappear from the media and the government's agenda, as if by the wave of a magic wand, with the help of a few days' worth of poisonous propaganda, at the utter lack of effort to identify and punish the culprits responsible for the Uludere massacre, at the deaths of gravely ill prisoners as they pass from our midst one by one, at the hunger strikes which have been happening for a month now, in which, presently, 400 prisoners in 40 prisons are participating, their numbers ever growing, at the members of the BDP being thrown into prison, including children and the elderly, by the dozens, their numbers having swelled to more than ten thousand. I look at those on hunger strike who, on the orders of the Minister of Justice, have been placed in solitary confinement in the Silivri No. 2 L-Type Prison and thus forced into a death fast. Why, I ask, is it that those circles we know to be democratic have failed to react, to take serious action aimed at achieving results? How is it that we fail to react to police attacks on every demonstration with a readiness and determination matching their own? How can the people of this country be so willing to live with this injustice and tyranny? How is it the willingness to live this lie reproduced?

The hate-filled, unlawful politics and warmongering that saturate the case against us are a perpetuation of the same language that has been used for so long, a polarizing language of warmongering in which the state claims that its actions are in the name of 'security' in the 'war against terror', a language which the state has successfully rendered as the dominant discourse. This case is a striking expression of the extremes to which the state is capable of going, feeding upon the mentality which defines as a terror issue the state of conflict/war that has been happening in our country in various degrees of intensity for decades, and which claims that there is in Turkey not a Kurdish issue but a terror issue. And it is precisely for this reason, that is, because it is not a singular/incidental case, because it is a part of the approach of the mainstream, which dominates all official levels of government, whether of the ruling party or the opposition, that all this is especially troubling. Categorizing stances on issues and even lives themselves solely within the framework of the 'war on terror', according to whether or not a particular action represents a 'weakness' in the face of terror, whether or not it will be beneficial for 'terrorists', and whether or not the person in question has ever given voice to similar opinions on any topic; this indictment clearly illustrates the aforementioned mentality, a mentality that comprises the greatest threat to peace, friendship, democracy and freedom in Turkey, and the greatest obstacle to efforts to resolve the issue. In fact, we might say that this is true not only for Turkey, but also for the entire world.

This case should worry not only us and our families, Kurds and members of the BDP, but everyone who still believes that another world is possible, who exalts the values of equality, democracy, freedom, and justice, and who envisages a peaceful world in which women are free, in which there is no tyranny of one gender over the other, which is respectful of humans and nature, and which embraces diversity.

In one of his essays, Eduardo Galeano writes that,

> 'in the schools in Uruguay, we were taught that the country had been relieved of the native problem in the previous century thanks to the generals who had destroyed Jon Charrus and his ilk.'

That is precisely what I mean by a security-centred approach; the same approach espoused by the Prime Minister [Erdogan] when he refers to giving precedence to citizens' security, not an approach which gives priority to myriad other concerns along with that of ensuring citizens' security. Trying to solve this 'democracy problem', which has arisen from what we call the 'Kurdish problem' but is, essentially, the failure to grant constitutional protection and thus meet the Kurdish people's demands for equality, democracy, and freedom, and the rejection of the Kurds' right to 'exist', by exterminating those who demand those rights: that is a security-centred policy or 'solution'.

There is an alternative to all this: a peace-centred resolution, an approach that, first and foremost, strives to identify and rectify the injustices and inequalities that lead to conflict and crisis. When problems reach an, apparently, unsurpassable impasse, and when deadlock reigns, or appears to, I believe that we must put aside all manner of prejudices, stereotypes, cliché words and thoughts, and review the issues thoroughly once more; that we must make serious efforts, requiring genuine labour, to listen, read, understand, and hear, without categorizing, labelling, or ostracizing, saying that this is so-and-so's idea. Every word which is obstructed or limited in its expression, and therefore fails to be conveyed or heard, every actor whose participation in this pool is obstructed, limits the possibility of an immediate, satisfying resolution. It is at precisely this point that we must defend freedom of thought and expression with no 'buts', not only for writers, artists, and academics, but also for everybody else. The ordinary citizen's freedom of expression is no less valuable than anyone else's. That is precisely the reason why the security-focused approach to resolution and the 'anti-terror' paradigm comprise the greatest obstructions on the path to peace, resolution, and democratization. We are not allowed to discuss and debate our thoughts and suggestions. Ours is a monologue, in which it is forbidden to speak in favour, but perfectly acceptable to oppose.

I believe it critical that we question this 'anti-terror' and 'terror-problem' paradigm, which is based upon a binary of those who are right and good versus those who are evil and, therefore, must be eliminated as quickly as possible for the welfare of all, because from the moment you approach the issue within the framework of 'terror' and 'terror issue', the entire axis shifts completely. Thus, we come to define the issue not as one that requires fixing, beginning with the very root of the problem, but rather as a menace that simply must be eliminated. Anyone who approaches the problem differently, who speaks out against the existing approach and against injustice, immediately falls within the ranks of those practising 'terror'. And so it becomes possible to criminalize them.

The election threshold [10 per cent for Turkish Parliamentary elections]; education in the mother tongue; punishment of security officers guilty of torture and rape; dam construction; inhumane prison conditions and the release of ill prisoners; empowerment of local government administration; whether or not to enter Syria; the subpoenaing of Hakan Fidan [head of Turkish intelligence]; all these matters are discussed within the same anti-terror framework, evaluated according to whether or not it will weaken the 'war against terror'. The widespread silence in the face of such blatant infringements of the right to freedom of thought and expression, and refusal to deal with the issue by means of political channels are, in large part, consequences of the perception of what is necessary and valid, a perception deliberately manufactured within the framework of anti-terrorism.

The minister, unjustly accused of impertinence, actually expresses the situation very succinctly, for he essentially explains the policy that is being implemented:

'The terror organization has another offshoot. There is such a thing as psychological terror, academic terror. There's a backyard that feeds terror … through painting … writing poetry … writing newspaper articles …'

The Prime Minister is quick to set straight the press and anyone who criticizes the KCK (Kurdish Communities Union) trials. He says that those who are critical don't know what it is they are defending, that they don't know what the KCK is, that they are not aware of the danger faced; and as soon as he says this, the number of questioning voices decreases. Rather than opposing the logic of the case, the absurdity of the charges and assumptions, and the fact that the case is based upon a presumed ability to read the intentions of the actors involved, we limit ourselves to vouching for those we know, and vouching that we are certain they are not members of an 'armed terrorist group'. We are unable to speak up and ask: what kind of an armed organization is this anyway, with no guns, no terrorist acts?

Those who know me and who know Büsra Hoca and Ragip Zarakolu vouch for us. And so the entire objective becomes that of rescuing the few people whom we know from these trains bound for Auschwitz. Yet what is really needed is to stop these trains altogether. These trains are full of people exercising their right to 'be' different, to think differently, act differently, propose different solutions. And the track that those trains are on is nothing less than a massacre of 'the Other' – an Other-cide. If we just stop and think about it, we'll see that, actually, all of us are on that same train.

In the women's struggle, we speak not of one group raising the consciousness of another, but of learning from one another and achieving a greater consciousness together; we speak, not of standing beside the victims, but of our common victimization. To me, this stance *vis-à-vis* life itself is extremely important. Acts of violence against women, murder, harassment, and rape do not affect certain women only. They happen to all of us as a result of the patriarchal mentality, with its passion for domination, love of itself and its power, and infatuation with tyranny; this is a mentality that insults and enslaves, with complete disrespect for women, whom it considers sub-human. We consider such violence an attack against all of us.

I believe it is necessary to assume this same stance not only when it comes to women's issues, but also when it comes to all other issues. It is only by standing up for the basic rights and freedoms of everyone from all walks of life, by standing up for peace and the freedoms of thought, expression, and action for all, and standing up against the imprisonment of voices, words, and language that we can defeat the dominance of lies and militarization, which impairs minds, dims consciences, and pulls wool over the eyes of all as it stokes the fires of enmity and polarization. The only way to counter this is, first and foremost, by repudiating and subverting the categorization of one side, the state, as good and just, whose every action is deemed right and necessary, no matter what it does, versus the 'bad guys', thought to be sub-human, whose words are not worth hearing, whose language is not worth speaking or understanding, whose human rights are not worth protecting, whose problems are not worth listening to, whose beliefs are not worthy of respect; those who are not worthy of living, whose deaths are not worthy of mourning.

I hope that some benefit can be derived from this damned trial, this unfathomable and ridiculous torment. I hope the fact that there are some of us on trial who are not Kurdish, and who do not fit the image of the Kurdish militant as 'bogeyman', 'sub-human', 'terrorist', 'monster', 'bloodthirsty', and so on, an image which has been created in the minds of people, not only by the existing AKP Government in Turkey, but also by decades of state tradition, will topple prejudices and stereotypes and give rise to questioning about what injustices the Kurds (those 'naturally born suspects', who have been struggling with the same problems for decades) face. I hope that this 'fate' we share, albeit only in small part, with the Kurds will help to make others aware of the importance of listening to what the Kurds themselves have to say, to their problems, demands, and suggestions; of the importance of bending an ear to this not inconsiderable portion of the population, certainly too considerable to be ignored, which states loudly and clearly that it imagines another, better future.

It is with these feelings that I convey my greetings, and call upon you to listen to the voices coming from the prisons, and to add your own voices to them.

In the hope that we will be together in days of freedom, which we create all together, with my love and respect,

Ayse Berktay Hacimirzaoglu

Please write to Ayse at:
Ayse Hacimirzaoglu
Bakirkoy Kadin Kapali Cezaevi
Kogus B-7
Bakirkoy- Istanbul
Turkey
www.pen-international.org

Liberty

I was quite happy in my new place, and if there was one thing that I missed, it must not be thought I was discontented; all who had to do with me were good, and I had a light airy stable and the best of food. What more could I want? Why, liberty! For three years and a half of my life I had had all the liberty I could wish for; but now, week after week, month after month, and no doubt year after year, I must stand up in a stable night and day except when I am wanted, and then I must be just as steady and quiet as any old horse who has worked twenty years. Straps here and straps there, a bit in my mouth, and blinkers over my eyes …

From Black Beauty *by Anna Sewell*
Ayse Berktay's Turkish translation of this
English classic has been widely acclaimed.

We the Peoples

Roger Waters

On 29 November 2012,
the musician Roger Waters
addressed the UN prior to
the General Assembly's
landslide vote in favour of
enhanced status for
Palestine as a non-
member State of the
Organization. This is his
unabridged speech. Roger
sits on the jury of the
Russell Tribunal on
Palestine, which held its
fourth session at Cooper
Union in New York City in
October.

Mr. Secretary-General, Mr. Chairman, your Excellencies, Ladies and Gentlemen.
Thank you for receiving me at this moment of solidarity and crisis. I am a musician, not a diplomat, and so I shall not waste this precious opportunity on niceties of protocol.

I appear before you as a representative of the fourth Russell Tribunal on Palestine and in that capacity I am representing global civil society. By way of preamble I should say my remarks here today are not personal or driven by prejudice or malice, I am looking only to shed some light on the predicament of a beleaguered people. The Russell Tribunal on Palestine was created to shed such light, to seek accountability for the violations of international law, and the lack of United Nations resolve that prevents the Palestinian people from achieving their inalienable rights, especially the right of self-determination. One particular stimulus to our convening was the disturbing failure of the international community to implement and enforce the clear judgment of the International Court of Justice in 2004, contained in its advisory opinion on the Israeli Wall, as requested by the UN.

We met here in New York City, six weeks ago, on the 6th and 7th of October, having previously sent out invitations to all interested parties. After listening to exhaustive testimony from many expert witnesses, and after careful deliberation, we arrived at the following judgments.

We found that the State of Israel is guilty of a number of international crimes.
1. Apartheid. The UN's International Covenant on the Suppression and Punishment of the Crime of Apartheid,

defines that crime as inhuman acts by any government that are 'committed for the purpose of establishing and maintaining domination by one racial group of persons over any other racial group of persons and systematically oppressing them'. As you all know, the prohibited acts include arbitrary arrest, legislative measures that discriminate in the political, social, economic and cultural fields, measures that divide the population along racial lines, and the persecution of those opposed to the system of apartheid.

As you are aware, this finding by the tribunal was endorsed earlier in the year by the Human Rights Committee's Committee for the Elimination of Racial Discrimination, in Geneva, after submissions by the Tribunal made both orally and in writing.

2. Ethnic cleansing. In this case that crime includes the systematic eviction of much of the native Palestinian population by force since 1947-48.

3. Collective punishment of a civilian population, explicitly prohibited by the Geneva Convention Article 33. Israel has violated its obligation as Occupying Power throughout the Occupied Palestinian Territory, including the West Bank, Gaza and East Jerusalem. Its most serious violations have occurred recently in Gaza with the blockade and virtual imprisonment of the entire population, the indiscriminate killing of Palestinians during the Israeli offensive, Operation Cast Lead in 2008 and 2009, and now the devastation wrought by the recent attack, ironically named, 'Operation Pillar of Defense'.

As I speak, I can hear the tut, tutting of governmental and media tongues trotting out the well worn mantra of the apologists. 'Hamas started it with their rocket attacks, Israel is only defending itself.' Let us examine that argument. Did Hamas start 'It'? When did 'It' start? How we understand history is shaped by when we start the clock. If we start the clock at a moment when rockets are fired from Gaza into Israel on a certain afternoon, that is one history. If we start the clock earlier that morning, when a 13-year-old Palestinian boy was shot dead by Israeli soldiers as he played soccer on a Gaza field, history starts to look a little different. If we go back further, we see that since 'Operation Cast Lead', according to the Israeli human rights organization *B'tselem*, 271 Palestinians were killed by Israeli bombs, rockets, drones and warplanes, and during the same period not a single Israeli was killed. A good case can be made that 'It' started in 1967, with the occupation of Gaza and the West Bank. History tells us that the invasion and occupation of a land and the subjugation of its people almost always creates a resistance. Ask the French or the Dutch or the Poles or the Czechs, the list goes on. This crisis in Gaza is a crisis rooted in occupation.

Israel and its allies would contend that Gaza is no longer occupied. Really? The withdrawal of soldiers and settlers in 2005 changed the nature, not the existence, of occupation. Israel still controls Gaza's airspace, coastal waters, borders, land, economy and lives. Gaza is still occupied. The people of Gaza, the 1.6 million Palestinians, half of them children under the age of 16, live in an open-air prison. That is the reality that underlies the current crisis. And until we not only understand that, and until you, Excellencies, your governments, and your General Assembly take responsibility to end that occupation, we cannot even hope that the current crisis is over. In October, on the last occasion jurors from The Russell Tribunal addressed this committee, we were assured that our representations and reports would be advanced on the floor of the General Assembly for general debate. If things go well today, we may hope to hold you, Excellencies, to that assurance.

I have diverted briefly. Let me return to the Israeli violations, which the Russell Tribunal identified.

4. Contravention of the Fourth Geneva Convention's prohibition on settlements – specifically Article 49. The settlements, ALL the settlements, are not simply an obstacle to peace; they are illegal. Period. Full Stop. All of them. You, in the General Assembly, and even the Security Council as well, have over the years identified them as illegal. And yet they stand, a daily reality in which now more than 600,000 Israeli settlers in the West Bank and Occupied East Jerusalem violate the law every morning simply by waking up – because their houses sit on illegally expropriated land. It is not enough to call, as some governments do, for an end to further settlement expansion; if we are to live under the law, the entire settlement undertaking must be ended.

5. Use of illegal weapons. During Israel's Cast Lead operation, four years ago, international human rights organizations documented Tel Aviv's use of white phosphorous in attacks on Gaza. Human Rights Watch found that, and I quote, 'Israel's repeated firing of white phosphorous shells over densely populated areas of Gaza during its recent military campaign was indiscriminate and is evidence of war crimes'. White phosphorous burns at up to 1500 degrees Fahrenheit. Imagine what happens when it comes into contact with the skin of a child. Human Rights Watch called for Israel's 'senior commanders' to be held accountable. But, so far, there has been no such accountability. No governments, nor even you, the United Nations General Assembly, have attempted to hold these Israeli commanders accountable. We hear a great deal about the UN's commitment to the 'responsibility to protect' vulnerable populations. Surely the UN's

'responsibility to protect' must extend to this most vulnerable of populations; Palestinians, imprisoned in a crowded, besieged open-air prison? There are more violations, your Excellencies, but you know that. Your resolutions trace the history of Israeli violations. You regret, you deplore, you even condemn the violations. But when have your resolutions been implemented? It is not enough to deplore and condemn. What we need is for the United Nations – for you, Excellencies, your governments and the General Assembly in which you serve – to take seriously your Responsibility to Protect Palestinians living under occupation and facing the daily violation of their inalienable rights of self-determination and equality. The will of 'we the peoples of these United Nations' is that all our brothers and sisters should be free to live in self-determination, that the oppressed should be released from their burden, by being given recourse to the law, and that the oppressors should be called to account by that same law.

In 1981, I wrote a song, called 'The Gunner's Dream'. It appeared on a Pink Floyd album, 'The Final Cut'. The song purports to express the dying dream of an RAF gunner as he plunges to his death from a stricken aircraft towards the corner of some foreign field. He dreams of the future for which he is giving his life. I quote.

> A place to stay Enough to eat Somewhere old heroes shuffle safely down the street Where you can speak out loud about your doubts and fears And what's more No one ever disappears you never hear their standard issue Kicking in your door. You can relax on both sides of the tracks And maniacs, don't blow holes, in bandsmen by remote control And everyone has recourse to the law And no one kills the children anymore No one kills the children anymore.

In 1982 and again in 1983, the General Assembly passed resolutions holding Israel accountable for its violations. Those resolutions called for a complete arms embargo and an end to military aid and trade with Israel. Those resolutions were never implemented. We never expected the United States, or my government, I'm from the UK, by the way, to implement those GA resolutions – the US is giving Israel $4.1 billion this year to bolster its already bloated military. The International Monetary Fund says Israel is the 26th wealthiest country in the world, and Israel is the only nuclear weapons state in the Middle East – why would any government be giving them money for more arms? Beats me. But the reality that they are does not excuse other governments from their obligations to implement those arms embargo resolutions. No such embargo has been imposed. Instead, it has fallen to global civil society to take the lead. Following a

2005 call from Palestinian civil society, social movements, activists, and, increasingly, church bodies, and even some local government authorities around the world have created the campaign for Boycott, Divestment and Sanctions. It aims, as many of you know, to bring non-violent economic pressure to bear on Israel to force an end to its violations, an end to occupation and apartheid, an end to the denial of Palestinians' right of return, and an end to Palestinian citizens of Israel being required to live as second class citizens, discriminated against on racial grounds, and subject to different laws than their Jewish compatriots. The BDS movement is gaining ground hand over fist. Just last week I was happy to write a letter of support to the Student Government of the University of California, Irvine, congratulating them on demanding that their University divest from companies that profit from the Israeli occupation. Also last summer, I was in Pittsburg to witness the Presbyterian Churches of the USA general assembly vote on a resolution to divest from Motorola, Caterpillar and Hewlett Packard. This would have been unthinkable ten years ago. To quote the great Bob Dylan, 'The Times They Are A-Changin'.

Back to today. You, the members of the General Assembly are about to have the opportunity to vote on changing Palestine's UN status to that of a non-member State. Whilst not according full UN membership, it would provide UN recognition to Palestine as a state that would have the right to sign treaties – crucially, including the Rome Treaty as a signatory to the International Criminal Court.

This is a momentous occasion, which was started here 13 months ago. It is one of those rare instances where you, Excellencies, can change the course and the face of history, and at the same time reinforce one of the founding principles of the UN – the right to self-determination. The bid implicitly incorporates pre-1967 borders, includes the integrity of East Jerusalem, an autonomous Gaza, and the refugee diaspora.

It is momentous because there are already over 132 members who have recognized Palestine as a state, and more are appearing every day. And, now, just this week, Hamas has lent its support.

I urge you to consider two points. Firstly, please resist pressure from any powerful government to coerce you into defeating or delaying this issue – sadly there is a history of coercion in this hallowed place. No government, however rich or powerful, should be allowed to use its financial or military muscle to set UN policy by bullying other states on this or any other issue. Secondly, do not take the statehood vote as the end of fulfilling your obligations – General Assembly responsibility goes far beyond UN technicalities. It must include real protection of Palestinians under occupation and real accountability for violations of the law. You have powers you do not use. You do not have to defer to, or wait for, the Security Council.

In just a few months, we will commemorate the tenth anniversary of the killing of Rachel Corrie, the young peace activist killed by an Israeli soldier driving an armoured Caterpillar bulldozer as she tried to protect the house of a pharmacist and his family in Rafah, on Gaza's border. International activists like Rachel Corrie, Tom Hurndall and James Miller took the risks they did, and they, and their families, paid the ultimate price, because the international community – your governments and the United Nations itself – had failed to protect the vulnerable Palestinian population living under this prolonged occupation. We are proud, though tears burn our eyes, of the work of these young activists, and deeply moved by their sacrifice. But we are angry, too, that our governments and our international institutions, including the General Assembly, have failed to provide the protection that would make Rachel Corrie's sacrifice unnecessary. Also, let us not forget the thousands of courageous and anonymous Palestinians and their equally courageous Israeli brothers and sisters in arms (boycott from within) who protest peacefully on a weekly basis for the simple basic right to an ordinary human life. The right to live in dignity and peace, to raise their families, to till the land, to build a just society, to travel abroad, to be free of occupation, to aspire to each and every human goal, just like the rest of us.

Speaking of the rest of us, I live here in New York City. We are a somewhat parochial group, we New Yorkers, to a large extent cut off by propaganda and privilege from the realities of the Palestinians' plight. Few of us understand that the government of the United States of America, particularly through its power of veto in the Security Council, protects Israel from the condemnation of the global civil society that I have the honour to represent here today.

Even as bombs rained down on 1.6 million people in Gaza, the President of the United States of America reasserted his position that 'Israel has the right to defend itself'.

We all know the reach and power of Israel's military capability and the deadly effects of its actions. So what did President Obama mean? Did he mean that Israel has the right to indefinitely occupy the whole of the region, that Israel has the right to forcibly evict the populations of the Occupied Territories, house by house, village by village? Did he mean that in this special case Israel has the right to carry out campaigns of ethnic cleansing and apartheid, and that the US will protect Israel's right to do so? Did he mean that Israel has the right to build roads, in occupied territory, protected by razor wire and concrete walls and CCTV and machine guns to protect the residents of Jewish-only settlements? Did he mean that indiscriminate and deadly bombing attacks, including the use of white phosphorous, on the civilian population of Gaza, by an overwhelmingly superior military force, is justified on the grounds of defence? The Palestinians are an ancient, intelligent, cultured, hospitable, and generous people. And, of course, they have pride and will resist the occupation of their land and defend their women and children and their property to the best of their ability. Who would not? Would you? Would I? Would President Obama? One would hope so. It would be his duty. Imagine Washington DC, walled in, a prison, mainly rubble from repeated attacks. No one allowed in or out. Constant power cuts, foreign gunboats on the Potomac killing the fishermen, warplanes launching surgical air strikes from their impunity on high, taking out not only the resistance but women and children, too.

More than a generation ago, the General Assembly passed resolution 2625, dealing with the principle of equal rights and self-determination. It recognized that when a people face 'any forcible action' depriving them of those rights, that they have the right to 'actions against, and resistance to' such use of force. When the international community does not shoulder its 'responsibility to protect', Palestinians will shoulder that responsibility themselves. This is not to suggest that I support the launching of missiles into Israel. The internationally recognized legal right of resistance means attacking any military target engaged in illegal occupation. But let us be clear, as we believe in the Law as indispensable and even handed. The launching of unguided rockets into Israel, where the most likely targets will be civilians, is not a legal form of resistance.

Many civil society activists – including many Palestinians and Israelis – are committed to non-violent resistance. The BDS movement, which has spread from Palestinian civil society to activists around the world, is part of that non-violent resistance and I support it wholeheartedly, but let us be clear that the disparity of power, and the reality of the occupation, and the response of the occupied is the reality we face, unless we find recourse in international law and hold all parties to it. In the meantime, let me try to dial back the rhetoric a little and address the 'Israel has a right to defend itself' claim from a legal and historical perspective.

Ex injuria non oritur jus. 'A legal right or entitlement cannot arise from injustice.' If we truly oppose all violence, whether by the occupier or violent resistance by the occupied, we must aim to end the root causes of violence. In this conflict, that means ending Israel's occupation, colonization, ethnic cleansing, and the denial of the right to self-determination and other inalienable rights that the Palestinian people are entitled to, according to the UN charter and other tenets of international law.

So to the future. Hamas, having dropped its original demand for Israel to be dismantled in the run-up to the elections, was democratically elected in January 2006, in elections deemed free and fair by every international observer present, including former US President Jimmy Carter. The leaders of Hamas have made their position clear over and over again. It is this: Hamas is open to permanent peace with Israel if there is total withdrawal to the 1967 borders (22 per cent of historic Palestine), and the arrangement is supported by a referendum of all Palestinians living under occupation.

Mr. Chairman, Excellencies, friends. We are all here for the same reason. We are all committed to human rights, international law, the centrality of the United Nations and equality for all – including for Palestinians. We are all attending this meeting on 29th November that marks the UN's International Day of Solidarity with The Palestinian People.

But it seems to me, our commemoration of this day is not enough. So, what else to do? The battleground is here, at the headquarters of the United Nations, and simultaneously in the middle of New York City, with access to the media. The battle is two pronged: to continue the work of informing the people of the USA about the reality of the Palestinian-Israeli conflict and, most especially, about the role of their government, the host country of the United Nations, using their tax dollars to fund and enable Israel's violations. To remind them of the billions of dollars in military aid every year, the absolute protection of Israel in the United Nations, in the International Criminal Court and elsewhere to assure its impunity for war crimes and potential crimes against humanity – to impress upon them, 'the people of the United States of America,' that these dubious attachments remain the centre piece of their government's policy in the Middle East.

Just as importantly, we must address, finally, serious reform of the UN. The UN needs to embrace a new democracy. The veto must be rethought, or the UN will die. The use of the veto as a strategic political tool by one or other of the permanent members of the Security Council has become outmoded. The power of veto residing in the hands of just five nations makes something of a mockery of the pretence of democracy, of the idea that 'the will of the Peoples' is represented here. The system is too open to abuses. The blanket protection afforded to Israel by the United States' use of the veto is but one example of such abuse. For instance, in 1973, it blocked a resolution reaffirming the rights of Palestinians and demanding withdrawal from the Occupied Territories; in 1976, another resolution calling for the right of self-determination for the Palestinians; and two resolutions in 1997, calling for cessation of settlement building in East Jerusalem and other Occupied Territories. There are many more.

I urge you, the General Assembly, to collectively work towards wresting the power back to the people in order to facilitate progress towards a more democratic body, better able to pursue the high aspirations of this great institution, to represent the will of the peoples of these great United Nations.

You, the General Assembly, represent the largest, most democratic component of the United Nations. The United States and China and France and Russia and the UK have no veto here. What is needed is political will. You can make decisions, and take actions, that the Security Council cannot, or will not. The United Nations Charter begins with the words ' We the peoples of these United Nations'. Not 'We the governments'. I urge you, on behalf of the people of your countries, on behalf of the people of all countries, in fact on behalf of all the peoples, of this, our shared earth, to act.

Seize this historic moment. Support the vote today for Palestinian enhanced observer statehood status as a step towards full membership. And declare Israel's continued membership of the UN to be dependent on reform of its illegal apartheid regime.

Vote: 138 for, 9 oppose, 41 abstain (including the UK)

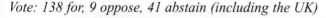

Roger Waters' UN address has received more than 80,000 hits on YouTube.

Nottingham Departed

Tony Simpson

... So I hold two fingers up to yesterday
Light a cigarette and smoke it all away
I got out, I got out,
I'm alive and I'm here to stay ...
Jake Bugg, lyrics to 'Two Fingers'

* * *

The new Clifton Estate, across the River Trent to the south of Nottingham, is under construction in the closing pages of Alan Sillitoe's less well-known 'prequel*' to *Saturday Night and Sunday Morning*. Brian Seaton, lonely soul, has returned to Nottingham, perhaps for the last time. He walks south from the Station towards childhood haunts near the river, and sees Clifton Grove and other playgrounds making way for thousands of houses which were to become homes for some 11,000 residents of what has been called Europe's largest council estate. For decades after the Second World War, Nottingham's reputation as a successful housing authority was based on large, publicly-owned estates built mainly on the periphery of the City.

Brian has recently returned from the British colony of Malaya, rich in rubber and tin, where, as an Air Force wireless operator, he was engaged in fighting local communists at the tender age of 19. In

◄ *Shirley-Anne Field and Albert Finney, stars of the film version of Alan Sillitoe's* Saturday Night and Sunday Morning, *in front of Nottingham Council House (courtesy of* Nottingham Post).

*The Open Door by Alan Sillitoe, ISBN 9781907869631, published in Nottingham in 2012 by Bromley House Editions, an imprint of Five Leaves Publications. The novel was first published in 1989. Bromley House Library was founded in 1816 as Nottingham Subscription Library, and moved to its present home in the city's Angel Row in 1822.

The Open Door
by Alan Sillitoe

In this brief excerpt, Brian Seaton takes younger brother Arthur (hero of Saturday Night and Sunday Morning*) on an outing to the countryside around Byron's ancestral home of Newstead Abbey.*

… In Hucknall Market he looked at the map. 'See that church?'
Arthur glanced. 'You shouldn't point at a church.'
'Why not?'
'Grandma towd me not to. She said it was wrong. Don't know why.'
'Maybe it is. But you know what's inside?'
He gave a horse-laugh. 'God?'
'Byron's heart's buried there.'
'Who's he?'
'A great poet.'
He bought ice-cream from a barrow. Arthur threw the paper down, licking before it could melt. They walked along a street of small houses towards the outskirts. 'Is the heart still beating?'
'I shouldn't think so.'
'Who ripped it out of his body?'
'A surgeon, I guess.'
'Was he still alive?'
Brian laughed. 'He died in Greece.'
'Did he fall in?'
'In?'
'You said 'e pegged out in Greece.'
'Greece is a country.'
Arthur looked at him slyly. 'Must be slippy.'

1949, after a two-year stint, he returns to England by sea, only to discover that he has contracted tuberculosis. Nottingham, in an earlier age of austerity (food rationing, in particular) under Attlee's socialist government, provides much of the backdrop.

Publication of this fine new hardback edition of *The Open Door* coincides with 'Saturday Night and Sunday Morning: the authentic moment in British photography', an exhibition inspired by Sillitoe's most famous novel and the grainy film adaptation directed by Karel Reisz, at Nottingham University's Lakeside Arts Centre. (Incidentally, the

University now has campuses in Malaysia and China, as well as the Trent Valley.)

The exhibition and associated programme of screenings and discussions of films such as Stephen Frears's *St Ann's*, a documentary homage to the city where the director spent some of his formative years (he has described it as the 'most friendly place in the world'), represents something of a step-change in Nottingham's self-awareness. Curated by Anna Douglas and Neil Walker, Nottingham people responded to a public appeal for photographs of their city in the 1950s and 1960s. Family snaps, all black and white, are interspersed with more professional shots, such as those of Roger Mayne, who provided the cover for the Penguin Special Edition of *Poverty: The Forgotten Englishmen* by Ken Coates and Bill Silburn, which itself forms a central part of the display, and was based on a pioneering survey of poverty in Nottingham in the 1960s. There are magnificent stills from Reisz's film, as well as shots of the filming itself, courtesy of the *Nottingham Post*.

The adventure in preparing this uplifting exhibition is engagingly described by curator Neil Walker in the catalogue* which accompanies it. Comprehensively illustrated and stylishly presented, Walker describes how his co-curator, Anna Douglas 'proposed a further democratization of our material by the inclusion of contemporaneous home photography contributed by the residents of Nottingham'. This is a very encouraging approach, which would be appreciated by all those democrats drawn to the Institute for Workers' Control and its famous conferences, many of which gathered in Nottingham, from the early 1960s through to Mrs Thatcher's arrival. Might that make a new adventure?

Like D H Lawrence before him, Sillitoe left Nottingham, although he maintained contact with family who stayed. Soon, probably, they will be followed by Jake Bugg, Clifton's teenage minstrel, whose recent hit record, 'Two Fingers', waves an unfond farewell to the streets that formed him. He is a refreshing new talent, nurtured by relatives and local schools, perhaps with some help from Bob Dylan's 'Theme Time Radio Hour'.

A step away from all these striking photographs, Nottingham High School (for boys) celebrates its 500th anniversary in sub-fusc fashion with a small display that includes the splendid seal and charter, replete with Tudor roses, from Henry VIII, granted to the widow Agnes Mellers to

---

*SATURDAY NIGHT & SUNDAY MORNING *the authentic moment* in British Photography, published in conjunction with the exhibition of the same name by Djanogly Art Gallery, Nottingham, 2012, ISBN 9781900809023, £15.99.

Saturday Night and Sunday Morning
by Alan Sillitoe

In this excerpt, Arthur Seaton takes a view.

'Once a rebel, always a rebel. You can't help being one. You can't deny that. And it's best to be a rebel so as to show 'em it don't pay to try to do you down. Factories and labour exchanges and insurance offices keep us alive and kicking – so they say – but they're booby-traps and will suck you under like sinking-sands if you aren't careful. Factories sweat you to death, labour exchanges talk you to death, insurance and income tax offices milk money from your wage packets and rob you to death. And if you're still left with a tiny bit of life in your guts after all this boggering about, the army calls you up and you get shot to death ...'

establish a 'free school' in the county town of Nottingham. Without apparent irony, this exhibition is called 'Balls, Boots and Players: Celebrating 500 Years of Nottingham High School in its Community'. Yet I cannot recall any opportunity or public invitation to visit the High School during 40 years in the city. Lawrence attended as a scholarship boy ('free schools', then as now, came at some cost), as did Ken Clarke, who came from the coalfield streets of Bulwell in north Nottingham. Jesse Boot stumped up some money, as he did for the University. Lawrence responded in verse (see 'Nottingham's New University').

In January 1963, there was an opening night premiere performance of *Saturday Night and Sunday Morning,* adapted for the stage at London's Prince of Wales Theatre. It starred Tom Bell, Joan Heal and June Ritchie, and was a benefit performance 'for the Bertrand Russell Peace Foundation in support of the people of Vietnam'. The Foundation was to be established that year. The horrors of the Vietnam War were still comparatively little known.

Saturday Night and Sunday Morning, the novel and fantasy, is a belter. The pace never flags, from the moment Arthur tumbles down the pub stairs in the opening lines, propelled by seven gins and 11 pints, until the closing paragraph, when his float bobs in the canal as he contemplates settling down with Doreen. Set entirely in Nottingham, it put the city on the map and encapsulated a way of life. The film, screened continuously during the exhibition, attracted huge international acclaim.

Nottingham's New University

In Nottingham, that dismal town
where I went to school and college,
they've built a new university
for a new dispensation of knowledge.

Built it most grand and cakeily
out of the noble loot
derived from shrewd cash-chemistry
by good Sir Jesse Boot.

Little I thought, when I was a lad
and turned my modest penny
over on Boot's Cash Chemist's counter,
that Jesse, by turning many

millions of similar honest pence
over, would make a pile
that would rise at last and blossom out
in grand and cakey style

into a university
where smart men would dispense
doses of smart cash-chemistry
in language of common-sense!

That future Nottingham lads would be
cash-chemically B.Sc.
that Nottingham lights would rise and say:
By Boots I am M.A.

From this I learn, though I knew it before,
that culture has her roots
in the deep dung of cash, and lore
is a last off-shoot of Boots.

D H Lawrence, published in **Pansies,** *1929*

In praise of troublemakers

Colin Firth

Colin Firth's films include The English Patient, Bridget Jones's Diary and The King's Speech. He brought to life eighteenth century England in the BBC's adaptation of Jane Austen's Pride and Prejudice. In 2010, there was a televised stage performance of The People Speak at the Prince of Wales Theatre in London, with The Unthanks, Mark Steel, Keira Knightley, and many more.

The People Speak: Voices that Changed Britain, *Colin Firth & Anthony Arnove with David Horspool, is published by Canongate.*

With his disarming title, 'An Eminently Skippable Introduction', Colin Firth leads us into a singular excursion through Britain's radical tradition. And what a tradition it is. From 'Disunited Kingdoms', commencing with the Declaration of Arbroath (6 April 1320), to 'Battling the State', which includes 'Pensioner Nellie Discusses the Poll Tax Revolt' (Militant, 1990). In the section on 'War and Peace', Bertrand Russell's letter to The Nation (12 August 1914) begins:

> *'Against the vast majority of my countrymen, even at this moment, in the name of humanity and civilisation, I protest against our share in the destruction of Germany.'*

This rich compilation resonates with awkward, resisting, oppositional voices who wrought change and did 'not follow a multitude to do evil'. In turn, Firth urges us to speak out, for 'democracy is not a spectator sport', as Howard Zinn once said. The People Speak is outspoken and thoroughly recommended!

* * *

Colin Firth writes:
If you studied O-level history in the 1970s, you probably know as much as I do about the achievements of kings, queens, archbishops and generals. My poor history teacher, Mr Cosgrove, occasionally used to try to liven things up by convincing us that they were all perverts. He'd bewitch us with extracurricular tales of inventive cruelties and obscure peccadilloes. It was often worth going to his class. This will have been offset with impersonal details of irrigation systems and mining utilities,

bridges and steam engines – anything that testified to Britain's industrial, commercial or military prowess.

But whether we were given the official versions of these stories or not, whether they were edited, sanitised, bowdlerised, bare facts or outright lies, something was always missing. While it may be true that history, by which I mean the one we're actually living in, is full of kings, queens and politicians – written by them or for them (they also have a popular place in film lore, I'm told) – the absent component always seemed to be just about everybody else. The further back one looked in time, the more 'everybody else' was portrayed as a homogeneous mass: the multitude, the rabble, the people, crowd extras.

In order to give faces – or, rather, voices – to these people, I felt I had to look outside the classroom and perhaps outside the country. I began to realise that many of the real stories of Britain revealed themselves through its guilty pleasures: the music I wasn't supposed to be listening to, or the jokes I wasn't supposed to be laughing at, or the books I wasn't supposed to be reading. Chief among the latter was Howard Zinn's *A People's History of the United States:* a book obviously not directly about Britain but which had an impact on the way I view my own country and the people who are left out of the textbooks. Zinn pointed out that these are the people who brought us democracy, that it works from the bottom up. That democracy's real protagonists are the troublemakers. He applied this conviction by living his life as a rampant troublemaker himself. And in so doing he changed a great many lives, including my own.

Another troublemaker, named Anthony Arnove, worked with Howard to develop that book into a series of readings celebrating the voices of such people around the United States. Aware of my enthusiasm for their project, they asked me if I would be interested in finding a British equivalent. This is the result of Anthony's and my exuberant and resounding failure to do that. In our attempt to include everything and everybody, we will have excluded whole centuries, whole issues, political movements, sections of the populace — and entire countries. There was a millennium or two to cover but we have to sign off at page 485. So, what we are offering you is a taster's menu.

I hope that these voices – whether they be socialists, anarchists, agitators, Chartists, suffragists, Lollards or Levellers – serve as a reminder that much of what we feel entitled to today, much of what we accept as civilised or decent, began as treason. Was fought for by men and women who weren't endowed with any political power, who were hanged for it, transported, tortured or imprisoned, until eventually their ideas were adapted to, adopted and handed down to us as basic rights. These freedoms are now in our care. And unless we act on them and continue to fight for them, they will be lost more easily than they were won.

Some of these words will be familiar to you. Some have been buried for years, words that might not have been heard aloud since they were first uttered. Some are the words of people whose lives overlap with our own.

Before gathering the voices you will encounter in this book, we had the great good fortune to bring together some of our friends and performers we admire to read a number of these selections on stage at a performance in 2010 that was filmed for and later broadcast by the History Channel. Some day, we hope a DVD of the resulting film, *The People Speak* (UK), will be available, alongside the film of the same name that Howard and Anthony made in 2009, with Matt Damon, Josh Brolin and Chris Moore (www.thepeoplespeak.com). This was not actorly activism: often implored to shut up about matters of consequence, actors were doing what they are trained and paid to do – act, interpret the voices of others.

It will not go unnoticed that, elsewhere, I have rather conspicuously embraced our monarchic narrative – and, in my haphazard professional capacity, also rendered the voice of a king. I can only say that I took great joy in the exercise and now revel in the contrariety. As Emerson would have it, 'A foolish consistency is the hobgoblin of little minds'.

Our exercise is a capricious one. We are not offering an objective version of history. It is not an attack on the many fine history teachers or their curricula (my father is a history teacher – the finest of all). It is simply an excursion beyond Mr Cosgrove's classroom. The pieces are chosen not necessarily because of their importance or because we feel any sense of responsibility, but because we liked them. Or they sound good out loud. We suggest you try them. We've cheated a little and added and subtracted from our event for the sake of shape. But not much. Vast quantities of rich and important material have been left out. Hopefully you'll feel indignant about that and feel impelled to point it out or, even better, compile another book … and then another.

Most of all, we hope you might find some inspiration in these pages to speak out yourself, and make your own voice heard on the issues that move you. As Howard reminds us, democracy is not a spectator sport, and history is not something on a library shelf, but something in which each of us has a potentially critical role.

The problem of China, revisited

Ben Thompson

Ben Thompson was active in European Nuclear Disarmament in the 1980s. He reflects on his long experience of China in subsequent years.

I first went to China in 1999. From autumn of that year until 2002, I was there mostly in the winter studying at the Beijing Language University and then, from 2002 onwards, I stayed there and made a living acting in TV shows and small films and doing occasional translation jobs. The acting was mainly for fun and also because it was a terrific way of improving my language skills and learning about Chinese history. I played many foreign devils of note, including Lord Elgin in the CCTV documentary about the Old Summer Palace (which Elgin burnt to the ground in 1860), Sir Robert Hart (twice), Lord Curzon, John Leighton Stuart, Norman Bethune. I played the German surgeon who operated on Field Marshall Liu Bocheng's eye, when Liu famously refused an anesthetic and counted 72 incisions. And I played many anonymous priests, ambassadors, crooks, seducers and Yang doctors. In the process I travelled to a lot of different parts of China and met a lot of people.

My problem with the commentaries about China in the foreign press is mainly that writers are obliged to massage their perspectives for the home markets they are writing for. The British mentality now seems to be painfully shrunk to a sort of 'health and safety first, big daddy will provide' perspective, around which the actual infrastructure of our lives is crumbling at an alarming rate. We can be in denial about that, but we can't seem to do anything much about it. I can't comment much on the American mentality, but they seem to think that the two words 'Tian'an Men' and 'Liu Xiaobo' say everything about China. In ten years in China I only actually met one person who had anything to say about Tian'an Men, (though, to be fair, discussion of Tian'an Men has never been encouraged much), but for most people it was one incident among many and was recognized as a mistake. Mao made much bigger mistakes, and nobody feels the need to pretend otherwise.

China is a lot less centralized than England or the US; central government has always played much less of a part in people's lives, and the country has always been run much more as a series of fiefdoms. A Chinese proverb says 'Heaven is high and the Emperor is far away'; another phrase describes a remote province as a place 'where the long whip cannot reach' and so on. And a lot of the deprivations which are ascribed by foreigners to Chinese citizens are actually not imposed by the government in any case, but by historical circumstances from which the government are trying hard to raise them up (granted that Mao, in his later years, added insult to injury on this front). Then again, many perceived restraints are imposed by the traditional family system and have nothing to do with government at all.

One commentator I would definitely recommend is Bertrand Russell. In 1922, he wrote a book called *The Problem of China*. It's a very perceptive piece of writing, especially given that the outcome of the struggle between the communists and the Kuomintang was not then assured. But one thing that Russell says which is most definitely true, still, today, is that 'in China public opinion is very important'. This is pretty palpable as one moves around China, and this is why the western view, that 'we have democracy and China does not', is a serious oversimplification. In fact, the Communist Party in China are responsive to public opinion and they must be, otherwise they can't retain their grip on the country. Just to give a couple of examples, when I first went to China an unmarried couple couldn't openly cohabit. People did it but they had to be very careful, and when the police came to our apartment, in 2002, they checked all our rooms to make sure we had separate bedrooms (I was sharing with two girls). Now nobody gives a damn, and this is because of social evolution. Now the website I used to find jobs and language partners has a section called 'Men seeking Men'. Nobody cares. Ten years ago the website would have been closed down. And there are many other examples from the fabric of daily life which show how people are quietly making their own history and creating their own future.

Public opinion is very important because Chinese people are very tough. There are no (or very few) government handouts, so people have to rely on family, friends and each other. And the government they have is not really a dictatorship, more like an oligarchy. There are factions within the Communist Party, and there are democratic systems within it, and different views emerge from time to time, often, as it happens, in response to public demand.

The feeling I got in China was that the country was being governed more or less rationally, under the control of a think-tank of some kind, unlike America, for example, which seems to be governed entirely by irrational fears and superstitions mainly steered by the right-wing press and various powerful military industrial lobbies. This is supposed to be superior to the Chinese system just because, every five years or so, people get to vote for President 'A' or President 'B', but as long as the combined power of the industrial lobbies and the media circus is sufficient to keep the turkeys voting for Christmas, it's hard to see what concrete advantages the system actually confers.

And then there is the banner-waving about 'freedom of speech', which mainly seems to mean internet freedom. And, yes, the internet restrictions are a bit annoying in China, though they can mostly be got round if you really want to. But, of course, 'internet freedom' suits those countries which are furthest along the slippery path of 'development' because they can force their standards on the rest of the world. The UK had theatre and literary censorship till about 50 years ago; maybe the Chinese feel that, at their current stage of development, there are some things they still want to censor? They are, in some ways, 50 years behind the UK, not necessarily in a bad way, but in some good ways also. When I went there 12 years ago, the first thing I felt about Beijing was that it reminded me of where I grew up in Yorkshire, 60 years ago. There were corner shops, the family was still important, people cared about each other and looked after each other. And, for example, nudity is still forbidden on the stage in China; it is forbidden in TV plays, very occasional brief nudity is now creeping into films. Most of the Chinese people I discussed it with, regardless of age, were against nudity in films and TV and who is to say they are not right? Why should actors (and it's almost always female actors) be required to strip to the buff in the course of their employment? And it represents a feature of Chinese society that people believe sex is for procreation and they have limited patience for the notion of sex as recreation. If so, why should Chinese people be forced by the Great God Internet to adopt contemporary American standards on these matters? China is a pre-Freudian society, hence the *furor* over Ang Lee's film *Lust, Caution*. Although, like any pre-Freudian society, it certainly has its seamy underside.

About three years ago, I was stuck in a place called Cui Heng, in Guangdong, filming a TV play about Chinese boys working in tin mines in Malaysia. This village turned out to be the birthplace of Sun Yat Sen, (briefly, in 1912, the first President of the Republic of China). My hotel was right across the road from the Sun Yat Sen museum, which included a large memorial hall full of photos of Sun and his associates and related historical figures, and also the actual house where Sun was born was preserved there. It was kind of comical to look at this house preserved inside the museum like a Fabergé egg, and then to go out into the village and see hundreds of almost identical houses with people still living in them, but that in itself was educational. It rained and rained and the mines we were supposed to be filming in were full of rain so I was confined to barracks day after day, and every day I put up my brolly and went over to the museum (which was free) and pondered the extraordinary life of this extraordinary man. One day I observed, in one of the pictures, a little woman who appeared beside him looking proud and defiant, like an alpinist hauling herself onto the summit of K2. Upon investigation this was Song Qing Ling. She married Sun against the wishes of her family when Sun was almost 50 and she was 22. She was the youngest of three sisters; Song Ai Ling married Chiang Kai-Shek's finance minister and became extremely rich, Song Mei Ling (the middle one) married Chiang Kai-Shek, and Song Qing Ling married Sun.

Sun himself is the most important figure in the development of modern China, much more so than Mao really. He was a truly international figure and lived in the UK and Japan amongst other places during his exile when he was wanted by the Qing police. He worked in the British Museum for three years, developing his theories. While he was in London he was actually kidnapped by the Qing and held in the Chinese embassy, but was freed thanks to the intervention of some well-wishers who, in the absence of any inclination by the British Government to intervene in the matter, managed to create sufficient pressure by means of a newspaper campaign to obtain his release. Sun later recorded what would have awaited him if he had been returned to Beijing,

> '...having my ankles crushed in a vice and broken by a hammer, my eyelids cut off and finally being chopped into small fragments so that none could identify my mortal remains.'[1]

A few years ago, I attended a lecture in Beijing given by Sun's great great grandson who now lives in Hawaii (a place where Sun had family connections). During the course of the evening he produced one of Sun's books and explained how Sun had planned exactly how the rail network in China would be developed, what the main ports would be, where the main trunk roads would run, etc. And he said that Deng Xiao Ping's modernizing ideas were all based on these plans and that the development of China's ports and railways had actually followed Sun's schemata more or less.

But back to Song Qing Ling; She is in many ways perhaps the most pivotal and most representative figure in modern China, she straddles all the ages of modern China and embraces all the tendencies. Of course, Sun Yat Sen established the Kuomintang, but he never intended it to become what Chiang Kai-Shek made of it. After Sun's untimely death, Song dedicated herself to upholding his ideas and being much younger than him she was in an ideal position to safeguard his conception of China at many critical junctures long after his death. Without her, Chiang could have claimed to be the rightful heir of Sun, but she stood up to him. She stood up against his cronyism and corruption and gradually, over the course of time, came to side more and more with the communists. Chiang at one point planned to have her killed in a fake car accident, but had to shelve the plan when he realized that if he injured her, rather than killed her, the storm of public opinion would wipe him out. There are many instances of her personally risking her life and her freedom in confrontations with Chiang. And she also exercised her influence directly because she was the sister of Chiang's wife (who, I believe, was not politically always in complete agreement with her husband). A few years ago, I played General Stilwell in a TV play about wartime Chong Qing, and I actually filmed a scene in Song Mei Ling's house in Chong Qing, where she lived with Chiang Kai-Shek. The house itself, though not large, is situated on the top of a hill in a beautiful park. It remains much the same as it was when Song Mei Ling lived there.

The point of this is that there is another book* I would like to recommend if you can get it, which is the biography of Song Qing Ling by Israel Epstein. Of course, many people will say that Epstein is biased as he was a communist and a sympathizer with China, but it's an absolutely fascinating book (quite long) and I can't think of one that better demonstrates the incredible scale of the country and the incredibly surreal nature of Chinese political life.

* *Woman in World History: Life and Times of Soong Ching Ling* (Mme. Sun Yat Sen) by Israel Epstein, New World Press, 1993

Note

1 This is quoted in the Epstein book. Epstein quotes it from *Sun Yat Sen* by Robert Payne, who had the quote from Sun himself, probably from *Kidnapped in London*.

How I Became a Socialist

William Morris

This essay was first published in Justice, 16 June 1894. It is reproduced in a handsome new collection, Poems of Protest *by William Morris, with an introduction by Michael Rosen (Redwords, 2013).*

◄ *William Morris's bed, which looked out on the final room of the Tate's stunning exhibition, 'Pre-Raphealites – Victorian Avant-Garde'.*

Kelmscott Manor Collection By permission of the Society of Antiquaries of London.

I am asked by the editor to give some sort of a history of the above conversion, and I feel that it may be of some use to do so, if my readers will look upon me as a type of a certain group of people, but not so easy to do clearly, briefly and truly. Let me, however, try. But first, I will say what I mean by being a Socialist, since I am told that the word no longer expresses definitely and with certainty what it did ten years ago. Well, what I mean by Socialism is a condition of society in which there should be neither rich nor poor, neither master nor master's man, neither idle nor overworked, neither brain-sick brain workers, nor heart-sick hand workers, in a word, in which all men would be living in equality of condition, and would manage their affairs unwastefully, and with the full consciousness that harm to one would mean harm to all – the realization at last of the meaning of the word COMMONWEALTH.

Now this view of Socialism which I hold today, and hope to die holding, is what I began with; I had no transitional period, unless you may call such a brief period of political radicalism during which I saw my ideal clear enough, but had no hope of any realization of it. That came to an end some months before I joined the (then) Democratic Federation, and the meaning of my joining that body was that I had conceived a hope of the realization of my ideal. If you ask me how much of a hope, or what I thought we Socialists then living and working would accomplish towards it, or when there would be effected any change in the face of society, I must say, I do not know. I can only say that I did not measure my hope, nor the joy that it brought me at the time. For the rest, when I took that step I was blankly ignorant of economics; I had never so much as opened Adam Smith, or heard of Ricardo, or of Karl Marx. Oddly enough, I had read some of Mill, to wit, those posthumous papers of his (published, was it in the *Westminster Review* or the *Fortnightly*?) in which he attacks Socialism in its Fourierist guise. In those papers he put the arguments, as far as they go, clearly and honestly, and the result, so far as I was concerned, was to convince me that Socialism was a necessary change, and that it was possible to bring it about in our own days. Those papers put the finishing touch to my conversion to Socialism. Well, having joined a Socialist body (for the Federation soon became definitely Socialist), I put some conscience into trying to learn the economical side of Socialism, and even tackled Marx, though I must confess that, whereas I thoroughly enjoyed the historical part of Capital, I suffered agonies of confusion of the brain over reading the pure economics of that great work. Anyhow, I read what I could, and will hope that some information stuck to me from my reading; but more, I must think, from continuous conversation with such friends as Bax and Hyndman and Scheu, and the brisk course of propaganda meetings which were going on at the time, and in which I took my share. Such finish to what of education in practical Socialism as I am capable of I received afterwards from some of my Anarchist friends, from whom I learned, quite against their intention, that Anarchism was impossible, much as I learned from Mill against his mention that Socialism was necessary.

But in this telling how I fell into practical socialism I have begun, as I perceive, in the middle, for in my position of a well-to-do man, not suffering from the disabilities which oppress a working man at every step, I feel that I might never have been drawn into the practical side of the question if an ideal had not forced me to seek towards it. For politics as politics, i.e., not regarded as a necessary if cumbersome and disgustful means to an end, would never have attracted me, nor when I had become conscious of the wrongs of society as it now is, and the oppression of poor people, could I have ever believed in the possibility of a partial setting right of those wrongs. In other words, I could never have been such a fool as to believe in the happy and 'respectable' poor.

If, therefore, my ideal forced me to look for practical Socialism, what was it that forced me to conceive of an ideal? Now, here comes in what I said of my being (in this paper) a type of a certain group of mind.

Before the uprising of modern Socialism almost all intelligent people either were, or professed themselves to be, quite contented with the civilization of this century. Again, almost all of these really were thus contented, and saw nothing to do but to perfect the said civilization by getting rid of a few ridiculous survivals of the barbarous ages. To be short, this was the Whig frame of mind, natural to the modern prosperous middle-class men, who, in fact, as far as mechanical progress is concerned, have nothing to ask for, if only Socialism would leave them alone to enjoy their plentiful style.

But besides these contented ones there were others who were not really contented, but had a vague sentiment of repulsion to the triumph of civilization, but were coerced into silence by the measureless power of Whiggery. Lastly, there were a few who were in open rebellion against the said Whiggery – a few, say two, Carlyle and Ruskin. The latter, before my days of practical Socialism, was my master towards the ideal aforesaid, and, looking backward, I cannot help saying, by the way, how deadly dull the world would have been twenty years ago but for Ruskin! It was through him that I learned to give form to my discontent, which I must say was not by any means vague. Apart from the desire to produce beautiful things, the leading passion of my life has been and is hatred of modern civilization. What shall I say of it now, when the words are put into my mouth, my hope of its destruction – what shall I say of its supplanting by Socialism?

What shall I say concerning its mastery of and its waste of mechanical power, its commonwealth so poor, its enemies of the commonwealth so rich, its stupendous organization – for the misery of life! Its contempt of simple pleasures which everyone could enjoy but for its folly? Its eyeless vulgarity which has destroyed art, the one certain solace of labour? All this I felt then as now, but I did not know why it was so. The hope of the past times was gone, the struggles of mankind for many ages had produced nothing but this sordid, aimless, ugly confusion; the immediate future seemed to me likely to intensify all the present evils by sweeping away the last survivals of the days before the dull squalor of civilization had settled down on the world. This was a bad look-out indeed, and, if I may mention myself as a personality and not as a mere type, especially so to a man of my disposition, careless of metaphysics and religion, as well as of scientific analysis, but with a deep love of the earth and the life on it, and a passion for the history of the past of mankind. Think of it! Was it all to end in a counting-house on the top of a cinder-heap, with Podsnap's drawing-room in the offing, and a Whig committee dealing out champagne to the rich and margarine to the poor in such convenient proportions as would make all men contented together, though the pleasure of the eyes was gone from the world, and the place of Homer was to be taken by

Huxley? Yet, believe me, in my heart, when I really forced myself to look towards the future, that is what I saw in it, and, as far as I could tell, scarce anyone seemed to think it worth while to struggle against such a consummation of civilization. So there I was in for a fine pessimistic end of life, if it had not somehow dawned on me that amidst all this filth of civilization the seeds of a great change, what we others call Social-Revolution, were beginning to germinate. The whole face of things was changed to me by that discovery, and all I had to do then in order to become a Socialist was to hook myself on to the practical movement, which, as before said, I have tried to do as well as I could.

To sum up, then the study of history and the love and practice of art forced me into a hatred of the civilization which, if things were to stop as they are, would turn history into inconsequent nonsense, and make art a collection of curiosities of the past, which would have no serious relation to the life of the present.

But the consciousness of revolution stirring amidst our hateful modern society prevented me, luckier than many others of artistic perceptions, from crystallizing into a mere railer against 'progress' on the one hand, and on the other from wasting time and energy in any of the numerous schemes by which the quasi-artistic of the middle classes hope to make art grow when it has no longer any root, and thus I became a practical Socialist.

A last word or two. Perhaps some of our friends will say, what have we to do with these matters of history and art? We want by means of Social-Democracy to win a decent livelihood, we want in some sort to live, and that at once. Surely any one who professes to think that the question of art and cultivation must go before that of the knife and fork (and there are some who do propose that) does not understand what art means, or how that its roots must have a soil of a thriving and unanxious life. Yet it must be remembered that civilization has reduced the workman to such a skinny and pitiful existence, that he scarcely knows how to frame a desire for any life much better than that which he now endures perforce. It is the province of art to set the true ideal of a full and reasonable life before him, a life to which the perception and creation of beauty, the enjoyment of real pleasure that is, shall be felt to be as necessary to man as his daily bread, and that no man, and no set of men, can be deprived of this except by mere opposition, which should be resisted to the utmost.

The Brotherhood

The recent exhibition at Tate Britain in London, *Pre-Raphaelites: Victorian Avant-Garde*, attracted huge crowds. An earlier revival, in the 1960s, firmly embedded images such as John William Waterhouse's *The Lady of Shalott*, Edward Burne-Jones's erotic Perseus cycle, and Dante Gabriel Rossetti's *Beata Beatrix*. Less familiar was Ford Maddox Brown's *Cromwell on his Farm, St Ives, 1636*, in which the Protector-to-be distractedly stares into space, white-faced, as his horse nibbles at the roadside, while labourers toil with saw and scythe. As well as Psalm 89, the frame is inscribed with a quotation from Cromwell himself, dating from September 1654, after the English Civil War: 'Living neither in any considerable height, nor yet in obscurity, I did endeavour to discharge the duty of an honest man'. Tim Barringer, in the revelatory and authoritative catalogue*, says *Cromwell* 'is the definitive Pre-Raphaelite history painting. Attentive to historical and local detail, it explores great moral and religious questions, combining past and present with Carlylean vigour.' Thomas Carlyle was a great champion of Cromwell who, according to Barringer, saw him as epitomising 'principled, anti-establishment, avant-garde rebellion'.You will have to travel to Washington or Moscow to see the exhibition, in 2013. The journey would be worth while.

*Pre-Raphaelites: Victorian Avant-Garde, Tim Barringer, Jason Rosenfeld, Alison Smith, Tate Publishing, 2012

This Morning's Surprise

This morning's surprise is how much I'll miss rail travel.
The green fields looming up and falling behind,
the milky tea wobbling in a plastic cup,
the engines steady vibration.

This afternoon's surprise is how many shades of red there are,
each one sitting in a room of its own, dense in meditation.
Each one a field of conflict, a medium of conciliation.

This evening's surprise is not that the novel ends
in a desultory return to the working week –
loose ends trimmed and tucked out of sight –
but the ferocity of my recoil
at the author's glib contrivance.

Midnight's surprise is Lorca's moon floating over Hackney
full-faced, round-eyed and speaking Spanish.

From *Street Music*
Poems by Mike Marqusee

www.mikemarqusee.com

Middle East Nuke Free

Yayoi Tsuchida

The author is assistant general secretary of the Japan Council against A and H Bombs (Gensuikyo) and a board member of the International Peace Bureau. This is what she said in Helsinki about how civil society actors can support denuclearizing the Middle East.

The establishment of a Middle East zone free of nuclear and other weapons of mass destruction has been a longstanding aim. The Nuclear Non-Proliferation Review Conference of 2010 agreed to convene a conference on this matter in Finland in 2012. Preparations were under way, facilitated by Jaako Laajeva of the Finnish Foreign Ministry. Then, in November 2012, the US State Department announced that the conference was postponed. At the time, Israel was massing its forces for another onslaught on Gaza. This onslaught was averted, thankfully, but the conference's rescheduling is awaited. Russia and the UK have called for it to be held in 2013, and UN Secretary-General Ban Ki-moon said he was looking for the conference to take place 'at the earliest opportunity in 2013'. Meanwhile, the peace movement stepped into the breach and convened its own conference entitled 'The Middle East without Weapons of Mass Destruction – the Way Forward and Civil Society's Input'. This was held in December 2012 in Helsinki, hosted by the Peace Union of Finland.

* * *

Now that 67 years have passed since the tragedy of the atomic bombings of Hiroshima and Nagasaki, young people who don't have any knowledge about these events have increased in number, even in Japan. 700 grams of uranium were used for the Hiroshima bomb, and 1kg of plutonium for the Nagasaki bomb. The volume of the explosives was the size of a table tennis ball. Such a small amount of explosives killed 140,000 people in Hiroshima and 70,000 in Nagasaki, by the end of

1945. Those who barely survived the hell were tormented by the atomic bombs' after-effects; many survivors died, one after another. More than 200,000 other survivors still suffer physically and mentally.

The Japanese people later suffered damage from the hydrogen bomb. On 1 March 1954, the United States conducted an H-bomb test at Bikini Atoll in the Pacific. Due to fall-out from the test, 856 Japanese fishing boats brought back radioactively contaminated tuna to Japan in the course of that year. Radioactive rain fell all over the Japanese archipelago. The destructive power of the bomb is said to have been 1,000 times more than the Hiroshima-type bomb. Radioactivity scattered by the test is estimated to have been 1,000 times greater than that of Hiroshima, though the H-bomb was called a 'clean bomb'. This is the reality of nuclear damage.

We fully support efforts to establish a Middle East zone free of nuclear weapons and other weapons of mass destruction. We think that crisis and opportunity co-exist in this region. The crisis is that, historically, this region has had imposed on it the causes of conflict and dispute as one-time colonies of European countries. Complex conflicts, particularly over Palestine, continue. There is some consensus, internationally, on the way to resolve this issue: Israel should withdraw from all the lands which it occupied in the 1967 war; establish the Palestinian people's right to self-determination; co-existence of the two states – Israel and Palestine – should be ensured; armed attacks should end; Israel's unlawfully constructed settlements should be removed. Occupying and settling in the lands of other nations is never permissible anywhere on earth.

At the same time, this effort should be pursued through peaceful means. Here lies an opportunity: in spite of long-term confrontation, none of the countries of the Middle East, except Israel, have acquired nuclear weapons, instead putting themselves under the obligation of Article 2 of Nuclear Non-Proliferation Treaty not to receive nor acquire such weapons. Against this backdrop, there is an earnest desire of the people for peace.

In 2007, we held an A-bomb exhibition in Cairo, and spoke with people from every walk of life including youth and students. What was most impressive was that we did not hear voices calling for nuclear armament and reliance on the 'nuclear umbrella', in spite of Israel's dangerous policy of neither confirming nor denying the possession of nuclear weapons.

We don't think this situation may last forever. That's why, as the Philippine Ambassador, Libran Cabactulan, then chair of the 2010 NPT Review Conference, said at the 2012 NPT Preparatory Committee, I want to remind you that, after Hiroshima and Nagasaki, the world was fortunate to avoid a nuclear holocaust for 60 years, and hopefully for many more years to come, but let us not continue to tempt fate.

We have to make known, not only to the Israeli government but also to its people, the imminent danger of nuclear weapons and urgent need for their abolition. Using all possible means, we have to call on Israel to sit at the same table with Arab countries.

The nuclear five (US, Russia, China, France, UK) are hugely responsible. In particular, the United States is to blame. While proposing a resolution calling for the establishment of a Middle East zone free of weapons of mass destruction since the 1995 NPT Review Conference, the US has prioritized Israel's so-called 'national security' over denuclearizing it. All parties should adopt a fair attitude to all the countries concerned. They should not apply double standards that defend nuclear weapons on one side while threatening such weapons on the other side.

In conclusion, I would like to make three points. First, it is crucial to encourage public opinion in favour of a total ban on nuclear weapons, which will surely contribute to establishing a Middle East without nuclear weapons. Creating a nuclear weapons-free zone is effective as a measure to ensure regional security, but it does not mean that nuclear weapons states can perpetuate their possession of such weapons. As a major premiss, they must abandon nuclear weapons. Nuclear deterrence theory is the main obstruction to a nuclear weapon-free world. Together with supporting efforts for a Middle East zone free of nuclear weapons, we, the peace movements of the world, bear great responsibility for putting more pressure on the governments of the world, in particular nuclear weapons states, to implement the agreement of the 2010 NPT Review Conference to achieve the 'peace and security of a world without nuclear weapons'. Such actions are needed before the next NPT Review Conference in 2015, and we believe that they will help achieve a Middle East nuclear weapon-free zone.

Second, as a concrete action, we plan to hold an A-bomb exhibition in Israel to raise awareness amongst people there about the damage and after-effects of the atomic bombings of Hiroshima and Nagasaki. I want to ask for your co-operation and help in realizing this plan.

Third, following the damage of Hiroshima, Nagasaki and Bikini, Japan suffered the tragedy of Fukushima, which is damage from the so-called 'peaceful use' of nuclear energy. We don't think the Nuclear Non-Proliferation Treaty is a platform for solving this problem. However, we believe that advances in the abolition of nuclear weapons will open up possibilities for new international co-operation, even on tasks such as shifting energy policy and eradicating radiation damage.

UTOPIA

Alan Kaczynski   **Let's Talk Utopia**
Ken Worpole   **Tolstoy in Essex**
Gillian Darley   **Moravian Graveyards**
John Payne   **The Putney Debates**
William Morris   **A Factory as it Might Be**
Colin Ward   **The Factory We Never Had**
Mandy Vere   **News from Nowhere Bookshop**
John Abbot   **In New Zealand**
Chris Moss   **In Paraguay**
Deirdre O'Byrne   **Woman on the Edge of Time**
Paul Barker   **New Lanark**
Dennis Hardy   **Catching the Bus to Paradise**
Paul Summers   **The Shadow of Chimneys**
Bridget Kennedy   **Keeping it in the Family**
Leon Rosselson   **The World Turned Upside Down**
Ian Parks   **Welsh Utopia**
David Rosenberg   **Freedom Without Territory**
J. David Simons   **Kibbutz: the Golden Era**
Will Buckingham   **The Trouble with Happiness**
Andy Rigby   **Communes Revisited**
Ross Bradshaw   **Down the Pub**
Jeff Cloves   **Stroud and Whiteway**
Ian Clayton   **My Grandmother's Kitchen**
Peter Preston   **Dreaming London**
Haywire Mac   **The Big Rock Candy Mountain**

THE BERTRAND RUSSELL PEACE FOUNDATION

DOSSIER

2013   Number 119

TRIAL OF KURDISH LAWYERS

Tony Fisher prepared this Trial Observation Report for the Human Rights Committee of the Law Society of England and Wales.

This is a further report on the trial of 46 Kurdish lawyers and other professionals on alleged terrorist offences arising out of their position as representatives of the PKK leader Abdullah Öcalan. The trial was adjourned from November 2012 and resumed on the morning of 3rd January 2013 at Silivri court. This report should be read in conjunction with my earlier report dated 8th November 2012 (available online).

Immediately after the hearing in November 2012, the hunger strike amongst KCK defendants had been called off. This had happened on the instruction of Mr Öcalan. In the days before the resumed hearing news emerged from the Turkish government that members of the intelligence service had been in further discussion with Mr Öcalan with a view to re-opening talks to find a solution of the Kurdish issues in Turkey. On the day of the trial itself government members visited him for further discussions.

After the hearing in November 2012, I obtained a copy of the indictment against the defendants. It is 892 pages long. With the assistance of two members of the International Action Team (IAT) of volunteer lawyers and students who work with the Law Society of England and Wales, a summary of the indictment and the charges against each of the defendants translated into English has now been prepared. This shows that the essence of the case against each of the defendants is essentially the same i.e. that in their capacity as lawyers for Mr Öcalan they effectively acted as 'mediators' who provided members of illegal organisations with 'information and direction' from Mr Öcalan and, as such, were involved in the 'strategy and management' of the illegal organisations. The indictment also gives further insight into the methods used to collate evidence, including the use of telephone intercepts, search warrants in relation to both office and personal accommodation, and detailed analysis of publications made and interviews given by various defendants to the media. Other forms of surveillance (including 'technical searches' making use of telephone signals to identify the geographical location of defendants) were also used. Items confiscated and examined included hard disks containing confidential client information with regard to other clients, together with their physical case files. These were also subject to detailed scrutiny in an attempt to secure evidence of the lawyers own involvement in terrorist activities.

Relevant Domestic Law

The main provisions under which the defendants are charged are Sections 314/1 and 314/2 of the Turkish Penal Code which read:

'314. (1) Persons who found or run a military (armed) organisation in order to commit the offences in parts 4 and 5 of this chapter shall receive sentences of 10 to 15 years in prison.
(2) Persons who are members of the organisations described in subsection 1 shall receive sentences of 5 to 10 years in prison.'

Offences under parts 4 and 5 are offences against national security, which would include becoming members of terrorist groups.

I understand (from research undertaken by the IAT members referred to above) that under sections 135 and 140 of the Turkish Law on Criminal Trials, the communications of a suspect or a defendant can be traced (subject to judicial authority being first obtained) whenever an investigation reveals good reasons to suspect that an offence has been committed and evidence cannot be obtained through other methods. This includes recordings of sound, audiovisual records and the monitoring of a person's behaviour in public areas. It appears that application had been made to judicial authorities to secure the necessary permissions for such monitoring to take place, although the authority given had allegedly been exceeded in many cases.

I understand that section 135 of the Law on Criminal Trials also takes account of the right to freedom of communication, which is enshrined in Article 22 of the Turkish Constitution. As a result, S135 imposes many restrictions on when and how 'bugging' can be used to gather evidence for a criminal investigation. These restrictions are based on proportionality and practicability and where evidence can be obtained by more than one method, the one that should be preferred is the method that is the least restrictive of the suspect's civil liberties. Thus, bugging can only be used as a last resort where there are no other possible means by which evidence can be obtained. Evidence obtained in this way can be used in a trial only if it has been obtained lawfully.

In these cases, the indictment states that a court order was obtained to allow evidence to be gathered in this way. However, the decision of the court to grant the order can be criticised. It is not clear that use of these provisions was proportionate (especially since it involved the breach of legal professional privilege between the lawyer and other clients) and whether evidence of alleged involvement in terrorist activities could not have been obtained in any other way. All of the lawyers argue of course that despite the methods used, the evidence obtained is insufficient to warrant the prosecution, and various applications were made, as summarised below, for evidence to be excluded on the basis that it had been obtained illegally.

Interview with one of the accused lawyers

On the day prior to the trial I was given the opportunity, via Human Rights Watch, of interviewing one of the defendant lawyers in Istanbul. I will not identify the lawyer, but the lawyer was able to provide details of procedures which had to be followed in order to secure a visit to Öcalan to take instructions.

The Ministry of Justice would only accept applications made by fax via a single law office, the office of 'Asrin' law firm. Application had to be made at least a month before any prospective visit. Öcalan is held in an island prison. The lawyers attended the police facility on shore at the port prior to the visit. Each lawyer was subject to some nine searches before being allowed on the boat which transported them to the island. The lawyers were not allowed to take any telephones, pens, paper or documents with them to the island. After a two-hour boat trip, there was a further wait during which each of the lawyers was fingerprinted and photographed. Allegedly, each lawyer was searched a further 12 times which included walking through X-ray machines and being scanned with other equipment. They also had to surrender any other items (even wedding rings were removed). Shoes were checked. The guards were all senior personnel not below the rank of sergeant or officer. All carried small automatic weapons. There were nine guards. They were then taken to a room which contained three desks. One desk, which they sat at, had four chairs. Facing them was another desk to which Öcalan was brought. Between the two desks was a third desk at which an official sat with paper, pencils, and a tape recorder which was running (they could see the red light). It was summer and very hot but there was no air conditioning in the room. They all introduced themselves by name and Öcalan asked questions about the current political situation and about the activities of the PKK. On this occasion no instructions were given but he clearly expressed his opinions and had clearly prepared carefully for the meeting. The lawyers were with him for an hour.

The visit was undertaken with the consent of the government (as, of course, all visits would have been). A note of the meeting was made later and stored with other records.

This defendant has been charged (in the same way as others) of committing terrorist offences. As with the other lawyers, all of the lawyer's electronic case files involving other clients were confiscated and examined without the consent of those clients.

The hearing on 3ʳᵈ January 2013

The hearing was conducted within a much larger court at Silivri than the court used in November 2012. There was sufficient accommodation for all relatives as well as the lawyers and the international delegation to be present at all times.

The timing of the hearing immediately after the New Year period meant that the international delegation was much reduced in number. In all roughly 20 observers were present from the United Kingdom, France, the Netherlands, and Germany. It appeared that the number of Turkish lawyers representing the defendants had increased since, in all, there were over 100 lawyers present on the benches reserved for defendants' representatives. On enquiry, we were told that all of the lawyers were representing all of the defendants. Similar security arrangements were in place as had been seen in November with a large presence of gendarme and other security personnel. Many were in full riot gear and had water cannon on standby. All those entering and leaving the court house were being filmed.

The morning session

The morning started with an application by one of the lawyers for the proceedings to be adjourned to allow the new law, which had been announced at the time of the previous hearing (to allow the use of Kurdish in criminal proceedings where the defendant wishes the proceedings to be conducted in their mother tongue), to be passed. This was rejected.

The judge then invited a number of defendants to come forward for charges to be read and to answer questions with regard to the charges against them. All save one demanded an interpreter and refused to answer questions unless one was provided. One lawyer, Umit Sisligün, was prepared to speak in Turkish and claimed that all allegations in his case file were untrue. He had been to see Öcalan only once and had followed the procedure demanded by the Ministry of Justice, had not been allowed to take anything with him, and the interview had been recorded so that the state was aware of everything that was said in any event. Further defendants refused to answer the charges in Turkish and there was a short adjournment.

Subesquent to the adjournment a long submission was made by one of the lawyers which focused on the lack of any 'rule of law' on the island on which Öcalan had been imprisoned. Reference was made to the fact that the European Court of Human Rights had found the mode of his incarceration in violation of article 3, and his isolation was made subject to an application to a domestic court to determine whether or not it was incompatible with Turkey's obligations under the European Convention on Human Rights. This had been refused. Attempts made to visit him had often been thwarted by representations that the boat used to transfer lawyers to the island was broken. Further representations were made concerning bail, and complaints were made concerning the recording of the interviews as a breach of client confidentiality under Turkish law. The hearing then adjourned for lunch and the international delegation were invited to meet the judges and exchange pleasantries. Opportunity was also given during the lunch break for the delegation to greet the accused but no effective communication took place.

The afternoon session

During the course of the afternoon a substantial number of lawyers made representations. Some made representations on behalf of all the defendants, some on behalf of particular defendants. The first lawyer to speak focused on the admissibility of the evidence presented by the prosecutor, and the fashion in which the investigations had been carried out. Her representations had apparently been drafted collectively by around 40 of the representing lawyers and in summary her principle points were as follows:-

● Privileged conversations between lawyers and clients are private and cannot be recorded under Turkish law. The privilege belongs to the client. Making a special case of Öcalan was not permitted and unlawful evidence of this nature should be removed from the files;

● In any event the telephone recordings made did not follow the procedural codes for the interception of telephone calls. There were 145 files of intercept evidence each of which contained over 500 pages of transcribed recordings. These should be removed from the files;

● Personal conversations between lawyers and their wives were included which was a gross breach of privacy. The contents of the calls were irrelevant to the case and only included to exert emotional pressure on the defendants and to humiliate them;

● Where privileged conversations between two lawyers had been included without the consent of the other lawyer (in relation to whom no authority had been obtained) they should be removed;

● Many of the recordings were of conversations taking place outside the time period for which authority to record had been given in any event and these should be removed irrespective of any other arguments regarding admissibility;

● No reasons were given on the authorities obtained to record telephone conversations. This was a requirement when such a gross violation of privacy, human rights, and professional privilege was being approved. Any such authority should be given as a last resort and full reasons given;

● 'Technical' searches – using telephone signals to locate individual defendants, had been undertaken without any permission having been obtained from a judge and any evidence obtained in this fashion should be inadmissible;

● After the defendants had been taken into custody access to lawyers and evidence had been denied for long periods and unauthorised intimate samples of DNA had been taken. The taking of such samples, which were not relevant to the charges under consideration, was illegal;

● Searches had been undertaken of defendants' offices and homes often in the early hours of the morning to cause maximum upset unnecessarily. Domestic searches have to be undertaken in the presence of another lawyer and this was not always respected. Much personal property was taken which was not relevant to the case. Often files were taken which related to other clients and when their return was requested they were handed over to the police so that privileged information was being given to the police rather than returned to the defendants; and

● Much of the evidence in the case files relating to conferences which the defendants may have attended, press coverage etc was entirely irrelevant to the charges and should be removed.

Mr Tahir Elci then addressed the judges. Mr Elci is the President of the Diyarbakir bar. He argued that the lawyers were not members of a terrorist group but were being punished for practising as lawyers. There have been problems regarding the Kurdish issue for over thirty years in Turkey. The government had just confirmed that they are having negotiations with Öcalan. In these circumstances criminalising lawyers who have acted for him was a breach of their rights. Lawyers are the most important protectors of the democratic state. They should be free to practise without persecution. There were many provisions in the Turkish constitution which negated human rights. Lawyers were equal to the prosecutors.

Mr Elci referred to a case that he and 15 other Kurdish lawyers took to the European Court of Human Rights after they had been jailed and tortured for pursuing cases on behalf of applicants alleging gross violations of their rights in the 1990s. They were in prison for six months and the European Court found that their rights under Articles 3, 5.1 and 8 had been violated. In this case the lawyers had spent an unacceptably long period in pre-trial detention and their rights under Articles 5 and 6 of the European Convention on Human Rights were being violated. Steps were being taken by the legislature in Turkey to try and reduce pre-trial detention and the judges had to consider that. There was also no evidence to prove that the defendants took Öcalan's words to the PKK. The government speaks to Öcalan so why should his lawyers not speak to him. There were many decisions against Turkey at the European level. Many of the defendants had come back to Turkey to face the charges and were therefore very unlikely to abscond. They should be released.

Mr Elci was followed by the President of the Ismir bar association and 25 other representatives during the afternoon. In this report I cannot summarise every submission but the themes followed those set out above. The defendants who remain in custody have now spent over 400 days there. Many advocates pointed out that their clients had faced previous charges in relation to the same interviews with Öcalan but had been on bail during the trials and had been acquitted, yet they were now detained pending the present trial whilst some of their colleagues had been granted bail. There appeared to be no logical reason why they had been discriminated against in this way. All of those lawyers who represented lawyers who remained in custody pleaded for their release. Many had come back from other countries (Iraq/Syria) to face the charges and were therefore more unlikely to abscond. No reasons had been given for the refusal to grant them bail.

Further representations were made with regard to the role of the police. In many of the European Court cases historically, the Gendarmerie have been referred to as the 'eyes and ears' of the prosecutor in Turkey. However, in this case it appears that police statements on case files go much further in terms of giving statements of opinion with regard to the implications of the factual evidence assembled. Complaint was made by many advocates that the police are attempting to usurp the role of the judge in terms of deciding the guilt of the defendants.

Others complained that the prosecution authorities had effectively made it an offence to represent Öcalan. One lawyer complained that after every interview with Öcalan the prosecutor had started an investigation. There had been over 100 such investigations which had led to many charges prior to the current trial, many involving some of the same defendants. There had been no convictions and, prior to the present trial, the defendants had not been held in custody. He suggested that the President of the current court had made rulings in previous cases that the recordings of the Öcalan interviews could not be used as evidence. What had changed?

Since the judge had indicated throughout the day that the court would finish at 5pm many advocates complained that they had to rush their submissions, some having less than five minutes to put forward submissions towards the end of the hearing. The hearing concluded at 5.50pm with an adjournment before a decision was made.

The decision was announced at approximately 6.30pm. In effect all applications made to exclude evidence obtained illegally were dismissed. The trial was adjourned until 28th March 2013. Bail was renewed for those on bail, and one further prisoner was bailed (significantly, this was Umit Sisligün, the only defendant who was prepared to answer questions and make representations in Turkish). The remaining defendants were remanded in custody.

It should be noted that the Prosecutor, although present in court throughout, took no active part in the day's proceedings.

Commentary

Observations made on 3rd January 2013, and the interview on 2nd January, highlight the highly unusual and political nature of this trial. Political and cultural issues are inextricably interwoven with legal issues, principles and procedures. All parties, including the prosecuting authorities, the defendants' lawyers and the defendants themselves are contributing to the politicisation of the trial. The collective decision to refuse to co-operate with the trial process by the vast majority of the defendants unless they are allowed to speak in their mother tongue, whilst understandable, is curious. All of them conduct their day to day business in the courts as lawyers in Turkish, and all of the submissions made on their behalf at the trial have been in Turkish. Whilst the struggle to pursue respect for the Kurdish culture and language is, of course, a very legitimate struggle there is a question mark over whether this struggle is best developed via this particular case. That, of course, is a matter to be dealt with between the defendants and their advisers. However in some ways it detracts from the other issues in the trial.

What has become clear, however (now that further detail is available concerning the activities of the Turkish prosecuting authorities) is that there are many aspects of the case which should be of considerable concern to the international legal community. The methods used to secure evidence in support of the charges against the lawyers raise very significant issues:

- under articles 5, 6 and 8 of the European Convention on Human Rights, (both in relation to the defendants themselves and in relation to the breach of confidentiality of other clients of the accused lawyers); and
- under article 8 (in relation to the issues which the invasion of family life resulting from searches of the defendants homes and intercepts of their private conversations with their families raise).

Perhaps more fundamental to the role of the lawyers who are charged with these offences are the apparently clear breaches of the United Nations Basic Principles on the Role of Lawyers adopted in 1990. These provide various guarantees for the functioning of lawyers the relevant sections of which are set out below:-

'Guarantees for the functioning of lawyers

16 Governments shall ensure that lawyers (a) are able to perform all of their professional functions without intimidation, hindrance, harassment or improper interference; (b) are able to travel and to consult with their clients freely both within their own country and abroad; and (c) shall not suffer, or be threatened with, prosecution or administrative, economic or other sanctions for any action taken in accordance with recognized professional duties, standards and ethics.

17 Where the security of lawyers is threatened as a result of discharging their functions, they shall be adequately safeguarded by the authorities.

18 Lawyers shall not be identified with their clients or their clients' causes as a result of discharging their functions.

22 Governments shall recognize and respect that all communications and consultations between lawyers and their clients within their professional relationship are confidential.' (Emphasis added)

There are also substantial issues surrounding breaches of domestic law for failing to obtain appropriate judicial orders to intercept communications, failing to respect the boundaries of the orders which were obtained, and also concerning the probity of those orders being made anyway. There is also the question of the length of pre-trial detention of all the defendants who are not on bail, which now seems excessive. All of these issues should be investigated and further monitoring of the trial should take place.

The trial resumes on 28th March 2012

JOURNALISTS ON TRIAL

Barry White of the European Federation of Journalists reports on an ongoing trial of journalists in Turkey.

Soner Yalcin, international journalist and owner of Odatv news web site, was released at the end of the 15th hearing of the Odatv trial at the Judgment Palace in Istanbul on 27 December 2012. However, he can't leave Turkey and he will have to report weekly to the court. He was first imprisoned in February 2011, along with nine other journalists working for the internet news site. They were accused of being involved in the alleged 'Ergenekon' coup plot to overthrow the government. The defendants have always maintained that the case was an excuse to bully independent and critical journalists. One journalist, Yalcin Kucuk remains in prison, along with former intelligence officer, Hanefi Avci.

As happened at the last hearing on 16 November, the day kicked off with a rally outside the court. There were speakers from the Freedom for Journalists Platform, the head of the Ankara Bar Association, a woman MP from the main opposition party, the Republican People's Party (CHP), and myself, on behalf of the European Federation of Journalists.

However, the situation soon degenerated into farce and 'low level' harassment. Our entry to the courtroom was blocked by security staff and we soon learnt that the courtroom would only be able to hold some 40 or so observers (families, supporters and reporters numbered around 80). In what is the biggest court-house in Europe, we were at a loss to understand why such a small room had been chosen by the authorities to hear the case. We concluded that it was all part of the harassment undertaken by the authorities to make life difficult for us. We further learnt that the judge had refused to allow all the defence lawyers, representing the dozen defendants, admission to the courtroom. I heard that some 17 were initially refused admission.

After considerable argument we were finally allowed into the overcrowded courtroom's public area to hear defendant Yalcin Kucuk put his case to the judge. But not for long, as the proceedings were interrupted by the remaining defence lawyers being admitted to the court. Then proceedings were halted again to investigate a possible breakdown in the recording equipment, which turned out to be a false alarm. After nearly one hour, Yalcin sat down, it was Soner Yalcin's turn to address the court. He was defiant and said that he was the victim of a conspiracy by those who allegedly had wiretapped Prime Minister Erdogan. Trial suspects also believed that incriminating documents found on their computers were sent by unknown persons via a computer virus, a point restated by Soner. After his twenty-minute address, he sat down to applause from his supporters and the buzzing court adjourned for lunch at noon.

Returning from lunch we found that the heavy security had vanished, but the courtroom was still overflowing into the outside corridor with people unable to get a place in the main public area. During the lunch break an overhead projector and screen had been set up for use by former intelligence officer, Hanefi Avci. He gave a detailed account of the way incriminating evidence had been placed on the computers. His background in the murky world of intelligence meant that he spoke with some authority on the subject. He finished at 2.15pm when the court adjourned for 15 minutes, at which point the lawyers took the floor for their submissions which continued late into the afternoon.

Along with Ercan Ipekci, head of the Turkish Journalists Union (TGS), I had to leave the proceedings around 3pm to meet journalists at the ULUSAL Kanal TV. Their editor in chief, Turhan Ozul, has been held in Silivri state prison, over 60k outside Istanbul, since 23 August 2011, also facing charges in connection with the alleged 'Ergenekon' coup plot. Ercan has done a great job in recruiting the staff to the union. After his meeting with them had finished I did an interview to camera about the current situation and the support the EFJ was giving to the imprisoned journalists. Turhan is being supported by the Swedish Journalists Union and his case comes up again on 10 January 2013 at Silivri.

On our return to the TGS office, we had a call to say that Soner had been released. It was from his partner Halide Didem, who was overjoyed and thanked the EFJ for all their support. However, the ten journalists have not been acquitted and, along with the two remaining suspects still in prison, they will be attending the Istanbul court on 21 March for a further hearing.

The next day we attended the court for the Devrimic Karargah case (which did not take place while I was there). We met up with a number of journalists and supporters from the previous day's Odatv trial including Muyesser Yildiz, who has been adopted by the National Union of

Journalists in Briatin, and her husband. It was a good opportunity to talk about the previous day's events and we parted knowing that we will all meet again!

Travelling back on the plane to London it was interesting to read in the English edition of *Hurriyet – Daily News* that the Turkish authorities had recently launched an 'information campaign' in capital cities world wide, to explain the reasons for jailing of journalists. According to the article published on 28 December, the Turkish Foreign Ministry and the Justice Ministry organised the joint production of the booklets which were delivered to each Turkish embassy in foreign capitals during the past three months in response to criticisms and questions about journalists held in prison. Should make interesting reading and shows that the campaigning is having an impact! Meanwhile the EFJ campaign to get all the charges dropped against Turkish and Kurdish journalists will continue into 2013. We are also concerned that a few weeks ago Prime Minister Erdogan called for a debate about reintroducing capital punishment for 'terrorists', a crime of which many journalists stand accused.

EYEWITNESS IN TURKEY

Tony Simpson of the Bertrand Russell Peace Foundation and Professor Patrick Deboosere of the Free University of Brussels issued this account of their observations of the mass trial of BDP activists in Silivri in July 2012. Subsequent hearings took place in October and December, with a further one scheduled for March. Many defendants, including Ayse Berktay, remain imprisoned.

A political purge is under way in Turkey. Since 2009, thousands of activists from the Peace and Democracy Party (BDP) have been arrested in police raids and interned in extended pre-trial detention. Following elections in June 2011, the BDP has 36 members of the Turkish Parliament, elected mainly with the support of Turkey's substantial Kurdish minority.

Now, a series of trials has begun. In the latest of these, more than 200 people are before the 'Tribunal with Special Powers', charged with support for, and involvement in, the Union of Kurdish Communities (KCK), which is a banned organisation. This grouping, it is alleged by the Turkish Government of Prime Minister Erdogan, acts as the 'urban branch' of the Kurdish Workers Party (PKK), also banned in Turkey because of its long-term armed campaign against the Turkish state. On this pretext, the Turkish authorities continue to arrest large numbers of activists throughout the country in regular raids. In recent weeks, prominent Kurdish trade unionists were detained.

Most of those before the court during the mass trial in Silivri are Kurdish members of the BDP, but some are Turkish supporters of the party, including Professor Busra Ersanli, the distinguished scholar and writer, and Ayse Berktay, the respected peace activist and translator. Ragip Zarakolu, a celebrated publisher of political commentaries and other writings, who has this year been nominated for the Nobel Peace Prize, was also in court, although he had been released from pre-trial detention following an international outcry. His request to address the court was not granted during open session.

Ayse Berktay has now been remanded in detention until the court reconvenes in October, together with most of the accused, although she has already been detained for nine months, since October 2011. On 13 July, the judges granted bail for an additional 16 accused, including Professor Busra Ersanli.

Our international delegation attended four of the eight days of proceedings in Silivri. The cavernous court house stands next to Europe's largest prison, housing some 11,000 detainees beneath high walls and dozens of watchtowers. During these days, there was time to read only part of the 2,400 page indictment to the court. On day seven, defendants had about an hour to make personal pleas, strictly in the Turkish language as the court refused to hear statements in Kurdish, although this was the preferred tongue of many of those in the dock. Sixteen individual defendants made such pleas.

Lawyers representing defendants collectively, as well as those representing some individual defendants, made submissions lasting about six hours during days seven and eight. Not all lawyers who wanted to speak had the opportunity to address the court. Those who did exposed serious inaccuracies and shortcomings in the lengthy indictment. The prosecutor spoke only briefly to oppose requests made to the court by defence lawyers.

The international delegation of three persons was excluded from the final session of the hearing, together with all the many relatives and friends of the accused. The reasons for this are unclear. We were therefore prevented from hearing the judgment of the court in refusing requests for release for many of the 200 people on trial. Apparently, the court, using some new provisions, granted only 16 more people bail, while many others continue to be interned, awaiting October's hearing. Why people are treated so differently is not at all clear, so that the decision appears somewhat arbitrary.

Based on what we heard in court, our impression is that the indictment is extremely thin. There was not one convincing argument supporting the heavy accusation of terrorism. The elements of the dossier that have been presented in court are mostly related to membership of the BDP, or to the fact that the defendants were attending or giving courses at the political academy of the BDP. We are astonished that the judges decided to keep so many persons in prison on the basis of the inadequate evidence we heard. There is no relationship nor proportionality between the facts as presented, and the extreme measure of keeping so many of the accused under lock and key for long periods. In Turkey, people may be held for up to ten years in pre-trial detention.

A similar and related trial of lawyers has now commenced in Istanbul. This will be followed by a trial of journalists in September. International delegations are attending.

The proceedings in Silivri were accompanied by massive displays of force on the part of the jandarma security services, replete with armed riot squads, two water cannons, tear gas, and Alsation dogs. Such intimidatory displays are certainly inimical to democratic politics, bringing to mind, as they do, modern Turkey's troubled history of repressing free and open debate. They also seem to reflect an absence of public confidence in the court. This lack of trust may, perhaps, be explained in part by a recent assessment of the Council of Europe's Commissioner for Human Rights, Thomas Hammarberg, who has characterised the attitudes exhibited by Turkish judges and prosecutors as 'state-centred' rather than rights-centred.

The House of Commons Foreign Affairs Committee in the Westminster Parliament, in its recent report on Turkey, recommended that the British Foreign Office should ensure that its Turkish partners are 'in no doubt' that the shortcomings in the Turkish justice system are damaging Turkey's international reputation and leading to human rights abuses. Such damaging conduct was all too apparent in Silivri.

Reviews

Rose-tinted Kosovo

James Pettifer, *The Kosovo Liberation Army: Underground War to Balkan Insurgency, 1948-2001*, Hurst & Co, 2012, 320 pages, hardback ISBN 9781849041874, £29.99

James Pettifer has performed a remarkable exercise in seeking to rehabilitate the Kosovo Liberation Army (KLA) from all the criticisms that have been made of it. This has required some major omissions of history and some even greater distortions. That anyone is prepared to read the story as it is told here arises from the fact that many generally well informed and well meaning people feel it necessary to justify the unforgivable NATO bombing of Belgrade and the appalling destruction it entailed, without any of the necessary authority of the United Nations for such an action. And this bombing became the precedent for similar military interventions in Afghanistan, Iraq, Libya and, it may be, Syria, without due UN sanction. The pretext for the Belgrade bombing was a supposed humanitarian need – to respond to a supposed 'massacre' of civilians by Serbian armed forces in 1999, under the authority of Serbia's President, Slobodan Milosevic, near to a village called Racak in Kosovo.

At the time, I read the many hundreds of pages of the official record of the trial of Milosevic, and I wrote it up in my book *From Tito to Milosevic*, published in 2005, which Pettifer quotes only from my description of Yugoslavia in 1919, not what I was describing of the origins of the KLA eighty years later. Pettifer does briefly refer to the military training of the KLA in Croatia and to its dependence on finance from the Swiss, German and US diaspora, but underplays the overall influence of the United States. Ambassador William Walker, who had managed the US intervention against the Sandinistas in Nicaragua, was the leader of the Organisation for Security and Co-operation in Europe's supposedly independent 'Kosovo Verification Mission'. Walker visited Racak after the so-called 'massacre', but he did not stay long enough to check whose the 45 bodies were, before reporting that a massacre had taken place. There had been a major battle between Serb and KLA forces, some of whom were not in uniform. Even Pettifer concedes that it was not easy to tell dead soldiers from dead civilians, but he still calls it a 'massacre', and Ambassador Walker's judgement has influenced the course of history. Forensic evidence from the Racak dead has subsequently proved that the vast majority of the deaths were typical of shootings in battle and not of executions, as had been claimed in naming the event a 'massacre'.

Racak can only be understood in the light of the extremely complex variety of national interests in the break-up of Yugoslavia. Germany was interested in its capitalist investments in Croatia; Russia saw Serbia as a Slav communist ally; the USA, under President Clinton, wished to retain its friendly relations with the Islamic oil states and Bosnia did have a largely Muslim population. That left Kosovo as a province of Serbia with many Serbian towns and villages, but currently a mainly Albanian Muslim population. In the nineteenth century break-up of the Ottoman (Turkish) Empire, Albanians had been divided by the European powers between Serbia, Macedonia and the state of Albania. Greece would not tolerate a united Albanian state on its Macedonian frontier. In this book Pettifer tells us nothing of all this background, although he teaches Balkan history at Oxford.

The 'liberation' of Kosovo from its position as a province of Serbia is thus presented by Pettifer without explanation of the large population of Serbs and also of Romas in the province, nor of the long history of the Serbian orthodox church in Kosovo prior to Turkish rule and to the conversion of many Albanians to Islam. In particular, there is no mention of the most famous Christian monasteries at Decani and elsewhere, with their beautiful icons, which date back to the sixth century and are the object of adoration for many Serbs. There is no doubt that Milosevic exploited the divisions among the peoples of Kosovo to protect his control there, but this history cannot be neglected in telling the full story of these unhappy peoples.

The divisions among the peoples of Kosovo were most clearly revealed in the international conference at Rambouillet in France, in 1999. This conference gets scant reference in Pettifer's book, and is not to be found anywhere in the book's Index, but its role is quite essential to any understanding of the rise to power of the KLA. Peace of a sort had been achieved in 1995 in Bosnia by the Dayton Accords, under the authority of Milosevic, and it was hoped by many that this could be repeated. The European Union had discussed plans for a European Defence Force, but this had been subsumed within NATO. Only the Organisation for Security and Co-operation in Europe existed, and the American William Walker was, as we have seen, acting in Kosovo for them. Madeleine Albright, US Secretary of State, was determined to try to establish US authority over Milosevic and his Russian ally. A confirmed pacifist, Ibrahim Rugova had been elected to the acting presidency of Kosovo, as something of a response to the KLA, and he had several talks with Milosevic, which Pettifer does not mention. Many observers, and I was certainly one, hoped to see a UN force on the job, but that was not proposed. Instead, an Anglo-French proposal of a conference at Rambouillet, supported by Robin Cook, UK Foreign Secretary, was claimed to be the only hope of a peaceful settlement. After much argument, an agreement was reached, establishing NATO's authority, and requiring both the withdrawal of Serbian armed forces and the disbanding of the KLA, but the Russian delegate left without giving his signature. Pettifer disregards the possibility of any agreement and assumes the inevitability of the subsequent rise to power of the KLA and of the high level US and NATO bombing, first of Kosovo and then of Belgrade, with all its terrible destruction of life and buildings, factories and services, with the aim of dislodging Milosevic.

The omission of Kosovo's Serbian Orthodox Church history and the distortion of the Racak and Rambouillet events are, unfortunately, not the only objections that I have to Pettifer's book. The role of the United States is further glossed over. There is no mention of the large US military base, Camp Bondsteel, established in Kosovo after the bombardment of Yugoslavia, or of the US oil pipeline being constructed through Kosovo to the port of Durres in Albania, with deep water for oil tankers to take delivery without the long journey round Africa to the USA and Europe. On top of this, there is not a word about the drug traffic through Kosovo, which Paddy Ashdown, who was there before going on, in 2002, to be the UN High Representative for Bosnia-Herzegovina, complained of in his autobiography.

This is a far cry from the heroic ending to his story that Pettifer quotes from a Chicago-based activist that '… a handful of people can do miracles'. And Pettifer ends his book with the words: 'Thus the conspiracy becomes the history and escapes the fictional' – just a pity that there is so much fiction in Pettifer's story.

Michael Barratt Brown

China

Ezra F. Vogel, *Deng Xiaoping and the Transformation of China*, Harvard University Press, 2011, 878 pages, hardback ISBN 9780674055445, £29.95

In the West, the view of Deng Xiaoping (1904-1997) is a matter of admiration for his conduct of China's economic liberalization and 'opening out' – in connection with which he is credited with lifting huge numbers of Chinese out of poverty – and condemnation of his order for tanks to enter Tiananmen Square, a decision which led to the deaths of hundreds, perhaps thousands of demonstrating pro-democracy students and crushed any dream of political freedom to match economic change. These days commentators are more ready to congratulate Deng on the the former achievement than they are inclined to condemn him for the latter horror, although in truth foreign investors rather quickly overcame whatever disgust they felt at the bloodshed of 4 June 1989. Ezra P. Vogel's weighty biography of Deng reflects this adjustment to a pragmatic line, with minute accounts of the domestic economic interventions, reclamation campaigns for the return of Hong Kong and Taiwan to mainland sovereignty, and foreign bridge-building of Deng's later career allowed to overshadow, in particular, his part in the catastrophe of the 'Great Leap Forward' (1958-1961), when an absurd Maoist plan for rapid catch-up with the West delivered, instead, death by starvation to tens of millions.

Indeed, the book is heavily weighted in favour of the period from 1969 when, in the midst of the Cultural Revolution (1966-1976), Deng was banished to the countryside for being a 'capitalist roader', through his uneasy return to prominence in the 1970s, until the period of his pre-eminence from 1978 onwards. Vogel affords just 34 pages to the first 65 years of Deng's life, suggesting the author's decision to downplay Deng's complicity with Mao's high-handed destructiveness, but also the phase of Deng's career as a revolutionary politician, which might have provided a view of Deng less familiar to Western readers. We are sped through Deng's birth into a small landlord's family in Sichuan, his time in France as a student and worker, which was also the major period of his politicization. Scant space is given to this latter process, as if the question of Deng's intellectual and ethical development could be taken as read: like thousands of other young Chinese, it seems, Deng simply became a communist and that is all there is to say about it. Vogel is not much interested in his subject's philosophical outlook, and it is true that Deng was a 'pragmatist' far more than he was a man of ideas. Still, the fact that Deng was among the millions of young people in the first half of the 20th Century who found meaning in Marxism surely merits a little more attention, as does Deng's role as a political militant and organizer during the war against Japan and the civil war between Communist and nationalist forces.

This biography is, nevertheless, an extremely thorough account of Deng's struggle against the legacy of Mao, Lin Biao and the Gang of Four to reorient this vast, poor country, in which, thirty years after the coming to power of the Communists in 1949, starvation was still widespread. We are given a full narrative of how Deng and his collaborators effected reforms of education and agriculture – ending collectivization and lifting millions of peasants out of poverty – and committed China to entering the modernity of science and technology, which was Deng's passion. Normalizing relations with Japan and the United States, countries to which Deng made celebrated trips in the 1970s, were also occasions for fact-finding about the developmental level of these advanced lands, which Deng knew, only too well, far outstripped China's own – a point that he never failed to hammer home to his audiences of Party and people.

At times, reading Vogel's book, one forgets that it is a biography, so concerned is the author to give all the necessary context to a life which is remarkable for its impact on hundreds of millions of people. This is to Vogel's credit, but it also exposes a problem with political biography as a form. To render the significance of such a person as Deng, one has to measure the circumstances of the subject's actions, in Deng's case, the party he worked in, with and against – Mao Zedong looms large here, of course – and the lives of those whom Deng governed. But this causes the reader to wonder whether, however significant this politician was, the proper area of focus should not have been the transformation of China, rather than the life of Deng. Vogel's study falls between two stools. When our attention is with Deng and his decision-making, the China outside of Zhongnanhai becomes abstract and blurry (although, perhaps, this truly reflects the view of the country from the protected vantage of the party's upper echelons). But when we are confronted with people responding to the effect of policy, for example, at the time of the Tiananmen killings, when hundreds of thousands of those used to being silent and accepting became vocal and demonstrative, one wants more of these others' subjectivity. There seems to be no moral or intellectual reason why we should not hear from the protesters themselves or those who can report on the people who were murdered. The book limits itself the point of view of the observer of the 1989 events.

Writing on 'Deng's Art of Governing' during the period of his 1980s pomp, Vogel records how, when Deng's office director Wang Ruilin gave account of his employer's views, 'he was very circumspect in what he said and avoided adding his own interpretation'. Roughly, there is a little of this approach in Vogel's study, which often seems content to reproduce the reasoning and outlook of Deng Xiaoping rather than comment upon it or add other perspectives, especially the perspectives of those outside the prevailing powers. Vogel is far from blind to the problems of contemporary China, including its grotesque, growing inequality and ruined environment.

Still, his work is far too admiring of a man widely lauded both within China and outside whose crimes it is now convenient and expedient to rationalize. The deeper reason for this may be the shared pragmatism of the biographer, his subject, and his successors about China's, and the world's, irresistible movement into the capitalist future.

Paul Brennan

Urban

Austin Williams and Alastair Donald (editors), *The Lure of the City – from Slums to Suburbs*, Pluto Press, 2011, 224 pages, hardback ISBN 978 0745331782, £60, paperback ISBN 9780745331775, £17.99

The possible future of cities is the focus of this edited collection of essays, concentrating on cities in England, China and Africa. The book also has chapters discussing more general ideas relating to city planning, the use of the past to secure attachment to locality, the use and abuse of public and private space, and ideas about the future of cities, positive or negative. Many of the contributors have been involved in the 'Mantownhuman' and Future Cities Project in England.

Although claiming that the book 'explores the paradoxes and contradictions, opportunities and challenges of an urban world', the chapters are an eclectic and, at times, confusing mix. The book is dominated by debates about architectural practice. They claim to be innovatory but the overall perspective seems to be individualistic rather than progressive, and at times patronising. The role of politics, social policy and geography in the growth or decline of cities is barely acknowledged in most of the contributions. This leaves a sense that, generally, the book represents a narrow, selective view of a complex reality.

Alan Hudson writes about the development of cities in China, especially the phenomenal growth of Shanghai, in Chapter Two. His particular interest is not growth in itself but whether or not that growth can be said to be 'dynamic'. He argues that Chinese Communist Party planning (especially within the five year plans designed for national, provincial and municipal government) and capitalist development (ring-fenced by the Communist Party) run parallel to, rather than in conjunction with, the people who live in Chinese cities. There is little connection between the planners and the people, whether they be registered citizens or recently arrived internal migrants from the rural hinterland. He argues that this creates a situation where there is potentially less trust or legitimacy in the system, the Chinese solution being to seek various ways of educating the citizen rather than engaging with potential contradictory behaviour or ideas. This is consistent with the apparent preference of Chinese planners for ecological views of city growth represented by the Chicago School:

> 'The human ecology of cities is proving an attractive area … since it allows the planner to retain the position of agent of progressive change, rather than ceding it to the less predictable citizen'.

The growth of Chinese cities is derived from capitalist 'surplus', which in turn is generated by the millions who have moved from the country to the city to escape poverty and environmental degradation. Hudson claims they have escaped 'rural idiocy' and 'the inexorable grind of peasant subsistence'. His concern is simply 'dynamism' and whether the technical approach of Chinese planners is enough to capture this. The prospect of working excessive hours in factories with very poor pay and conditions is not addressed, but this is a feature of Chinese society challenging the legitimacy of current Communist Party priorities (and any of Hudson's ideas about 'dynamism' too).

Dynamism in cities in the 'West' and Africa, comparing the growth of nineteenth-century London with that of twenty-first century Nairobi, is the underlying theme of Chapter Three. Alistair Donald's concern seems to be that 'modernisation' (of infrastructure, facilities and housing) is being denied or restricted in the emergent cities of Africa. Ambivalence and anxiety mark western donor countries' attitudes to the phenomenal growth of African cities, not least because of their burgeoning slums. Donald himself seems ambivalent: on the one hand condemning them (the dynamism of the city has passed these areas by) but on the other lauding the resilience of people forced to survive them (they have the determination to make a better life for themselves). The contrast between China (where the Communist Party ring-fences and uses capitalist surplus within the country) and Africa (where multinationals siphon off surplus for their own competitive advantage in a global economy) is not explored.

Throughout the book there is very little analysis of the impact of global finance on city development and the impact of neo-liberal ideas on the role of the state. The emphasis throughout is that of architectural practice and the apparent lack of vision current in the West, evident when comparisons are made with China and Africa today, or with London, Paris or New York in the past or, at a more current detailed level, in relation to ideas about overcrowding, planning, the use of the past to create new city landscapes, and the control of movement by humans and by cars. Much of this writing is descriptive rather than analytical, using an eclectic variety of sources, which sometimes inadequately justify some very strongly worded opinions. Some comments are simply offensive. For example, in a discussion of 'false urban memory syndrome' in a chapter on the 'historic' city, Steve Nash and Austin Williams claim that

> 'a heightened awareness of the past is symptomatic of those with little or no future. Pensioners or the terminally ill are at liberty to reminisce, but the fact that the country [the UK] is engaged in the equivalent of looking back to the good old days is a little tragic ...'

This is a good example of breathtaking professional arrogance, given the enormous shift in emphasis from the state to the 'market' and the impact of globalisation, which has had a devastating impact on people and places in the last thirty years.

Although references to Engels, Lefebre and Marx are scattered throughout the book, it is difficult to pin down the politics underlying this writing. The contributors seem to be longing for an uncomplicated professional autonomy uncluttered by 'green' or 'sustainable' restrictions. Similarly, their focus is not about achieving social justice. For example, there is very little reference to the Coalition Government's austerity programme in the UK and its impact on the construction industry or people needing homes. In Chapter Three on overcrowding, Patrick Hayes makes passing mention to cuts in housing benefit in the UK for those who are considered by the government to have too many bedrooms. Instead of detailed discussion of the impacts of this measure on place and space (surely architectural concerns) there is

> '... welfare benefit cuts may force "oversized" families out of London [but] the government's pragmatic use of size limits should not be seen as a Chinese-style limit on population.'

On the contrary, the Coalition's intention is far from pragmatic, and Hayes misunderstands the impact of these measures, too. In the private rented sector, 90,000 tenants have been affected already. From April 2013, in the social rented sector it is estimated that 670,000 will be affected with the worst hit areas in Yorkshire, the Midlands and London (where the poorest tenants will have to move or find money to make up the rent from funds supposed to be used for food and fuel.)

For anyone interested in a broader conception of the significance of the city, David Harvey has written about 'the right to the city' (*New Left Review*, 53, September-October 2008.) While agreeing that 'cities have arisen through geographical and social concentrations of surplus product' and that 'urbanisation has always been a class phenomenon', he analyses the impact of capitalist development historically (including in relation to global financial capital) and the material, financial and emotional dispossession currently being inflicted on the poorest in different countries including those mentioned in *The Lure of the City*. Instead of 'dynamism', Harvey's focus is on 'the right to the city'; a political slogan which foregrounds the significance of the establishment or reinstatement of democratic control over urbanisation in all of its guises. As he points out, Lefebre was right: the revolution has to be urban. The problem with the contributors to *The Lure of the City* is that they have a completely different future in mind.

Cathy Davis

Quite a Character

Roger Seifert and Tom Sibley, *Revolutionary Communist at Work – A Political Biography of Bert Ramelson*, Lawrence & Wishart, 2011, 414 pages, paperback ISBN 9781907103414, £25.00

Bert Ramelson (Baruch Rahmilevich Mendelson) was born in the ghetto of Cherkassy, a small town in the Ukraine, but in 1922, at the age of 12, he emigrated with his family to Canada. Showing aptitude at school, he enrolled at Alberta University and gained a law degree, but left Canada to work on a kibbutz in Palestine, before joining the Communist Party and the International Brigade in Spain, where he was wounded twice. After Spain he moved to Yorkshire where he was active in the trade union USDAW before being drafted into the army, in 1941, to fight in the Western Desert where he was captured near Tobruk. He spent the rest of the war as a prisoner of war or waiting for demob in India but put the time to good use, as many other socialists did, finding it a fertile ground for the dissemination of radical ideas. After the army it comes as no surprise to see him enthusiastically accepting the full-time Communist Party post of Leeds Area Secretary and going on to become Yorkshire District Secretary in 1953. This official position meant that he was at the forefront of the Party's industrial activities (second only to the Party's National Industrial Organiser, Peter Kerrigan) whose position he filled on the latter's retirement in 1965.

The book records some of the Party's, and Ramelson's, activities in the

Yorkshire period, mentioning a number of key rank and file militants, amongst them the redoubtable future Labour MP and advocate of workers' control, Joan Maynard. Worthy of special note is the authors' claim that Ramelson was responsible (together with his young YCL protégé, Arthur Scargill) both for the leftward shift of the Yorkshire NUM and the innovation of 'flying pickets'. Ramelson's activities in Yorkshire coincided with what the book terms the *'annus horribilis'* – 1956 and the bloody suppression of the Hungarian uprising by Soviet forces. In the context of this maelstrom, and given Ramelson's leadership position, the authors are at pains to demonstrate that Ramelson was no 'dull apparatchik'. The authors give an account of the case of *The Reasoner,* an unofficial dissident journal circulated in the Party, and edited by E P Thompson and John Saville. Ramelson's handling of the matter, according to the text, did show some sensitivity. It was settled without expulsions – both Thompson and Saville resigned from the Party – leaving on reasonably cordial terms, with Ramelson at least.

The year 1956 was a very difficult year for Ramelson, at a personal level as well as politically. When living in the Ukraine he was influenced by his 'Red Professor' elder sister Rosa, who remained in the Soviet Union. It was not until 1956, on a visit to Moscow, that he would meet her again, to discover that she had spent 20 years in the Gulag and her husband, also a committed communist, had died in the camps. Ramelson, however, whatever his personal feelings, still defended the Party line with 'gusto'. He obviously felt that whatever concerns Party members had about events in the Soviet bloc should be overridden by the necessity of remaining united. It is, unfortunately, all too easy to see that the failure to criticise fully the Soviet Union at this point lost the Party some 20% of its membership, and a whole group of its ablest minds. This contributed to its continuing marginalisation till dissolution in 1991. The text has Ramelson edging towards dissidence over quite a long period, certainly in relation to the doctrine of democratic centralism, but it comes with no satisfaction to have to say that, as with so many Party members, it was too little too late.

Ramelson's tenure as National Industrial Organiser corresponded with one of the most turbulent periods of British labour and political relations. The chapters in this book dealing with the battles of the 1960s and 70s are definitely the most pertinent and provoking sections of the book. He quickly established himself as a prominent figure on the national labour scene, thanks in part to the kind offices of Prime Minister Harold Wilson, who named him as the *éminence grise* behind the 1966 Seamen's Strike. The events of the period are discussed in some detail, outlining

Ramelson's often timely interventions, together with criticism of the non-communist left, justified and unjustified. The trade unions, and Ramelson to a large extent, were necessarily caught up in defensive struggles as legal encroachments were initiated to curtail trade union power. Defensive actions are, unfortunately, often defeated, and the opportunity was missed for a more creative and structurally incisive strategy based on workers' control. This strategy was misunderstood by many on the Left, partly because of the obvious dangers of co-option, but regrettably the oppositionists included Ramelson, who debated the issue with leading members of the Institute for Workers' Control (IWC) in the pages of *Marxism Today*. In this context, the book is insistent that Ramelson's tactical approach was different from his predecessor, Peter Kerrigan, and for that matter the Party leadership in general, when it came to directing the Party's industrial members. His was a non-authoritarian approach, which set the ideological direction rather than the organisational particularities. The book discusses his role in the debate on workers' control and his criticisms of the IWC and it does, in fact, make some fleeting criticism to the effect that he failed 'to give positive leadership on the issue'. The defensive battle par excellence was, of course, the 1984-5 miners' strike led by Arthur Scargill and, as the text makes clear, he and Ramelson had a long association stretching back to the 1950s. Ramelson's last direct intervention in an industrial dispute comes when he is brought out of retirement, six months into the strike, to try and persuade Scargill to soften his negotiating stance on pit closures to avoid a comprehensive defeat, but Scargill was pointedly dismissive.

Ramelson retired as National Industrial Organiser in 1977, but still worked full-time for the Party without a particular brief until he became the Party's representative on the editorial board of *World Marxist Review*. The latter duty meant that one week a month he would spend in Prague where the editorial committee was based. He cannot have failed to notice the dismal and repressive aspects of life in Czechoslovakia at that time, especially when pointed out by his ex-professorial window cleaner and former member of the Communist Party of Czechoslovakia's Executive Committee. Increasingly, according to the book, he became more and more critical of aspects of communist practice and doctrine, whether in the Soviet bloc or emanating from the now distinctly Euro-communist leadership of the Communist Party of Great Britain.

The book sheds an interesting, if partisan, light upon the bitter struggle between the 'neo-Gramscian' Party hierarchy and the *Morning Star*. Ramelson's allegiance was still to the policies spelt out in the *British Road to Socialism*, and he was firmly opposed to the new ideas emanating from such as Dave Purdy and Martin Jacques. He did not, however, play a central role in the dispute and the final schism, perhaps due to age and ill health and, when the Party was dissolved, Ramelson did not formally join any of the splinter groups.

Revolutionary Communist at Work has a certain pathos, as many of the causes Ramelson was associated with, or actively initiated, ended in final defeat. The industrial struggles of the 1970s ended with the cataclysm of Thatcher, and the 'socialist states' disappeared amidst scenes of capitalist plunder and jubilation. Of course, the book does over-egg the pudding a little when it comes to his role, and probably tries to make him appear, perhaps a more independent figure within the Party than he was. It does also make an effort to both defend him from accusations of a highly contentious nature, and to mount a generalised defence of Party members who were not 'complicit in Stalinism's crimes against humanity'. The book gets a few dates wrong and chronologically it can be quite confusing but it still remains a stimulating retrospective look at some of the events that shaped our present, both nationally and internationally. The one thing that does come out of the book is Ramelson's formidable personality. He was a vigorous and accomplished orator, convivial in manner, knowledgeable and still committed to an optimistic Marxist vision of the possibilities for socialism – and obviously quite a character.

John Daniels

Frank Thompson

Peter J. Conradi, *A Very English Hero: The Making of Frank Thompson*, Bloomsbury 2012, 432 pages, hardback ISBN 9781408802434, £18.99

I was at the Dragon School in Oxford with Frank, two years younger than me, and I kept in touch with him and his younger brother Edward in the holidays when Frank went to Winchester. But our most memorable meeting was a few days after the Second World War was declared in September 1939. I had met with some pacifist friends at a favourite student café in Oxford to discuss a letter I had received from Michael Rowntree telling me that his father, Arnold Rowntree, and Paul Cadbury had decided to re-form the Friends Ambulance Unit. I had agreed with Michael to join, and was supported by David Caulkin. Frank burst in on our meeting, slightly drunk, and told us that we were all wrong. The Nazis and fascism had to be destroyed, he said, and communism rescued from the Stalin-Hitler Pact of 1939. Frank already called himself a communist.

Frank told us that he was going to join up. When we said that he was too young, he replied that he would give a false date of birth. Whatever he said, he did get into the army and was very soon commissioned and joined an intelligence unit, called 'Phantom', and then the Special Operations Executive (SOE), a somewhat more open intelligence organisation. He served first in Sicily, then with the Yugoslav Partisans, and from them joined the resistance in Bulgaria, where he was captured and executed in 1944. Frank's brother Edward and their mother wrote a memorial of Frank, entitled *There is a Spirit in Europe*, a phrase taken from a poem by Frank. I sent my father this tribute in 1947, to help to explain my own desertion of Quakerism for communism. It lay by my father's bedside, when my father died in that year.

There have been several books about Frank Thompson, notably Conradi's biography of Iris Murdoch, Frank's great love, and his collection of the letters of Iris Murdoch, and the collection of Frank's poems made by Dorothy Thompson. But this book is even more deeply researched, and seeks to explain, as the title suggests, what made this 'very English hero'. Home and schools must account for much. Frank's father's love of India, where he had been a missionary, left a lasting impression, but the loving care of Frank's mother, Theo, must be recognised as central. Of his friends, Iris Murdoch stands out, and when Iris retired to her studies, Desiree Cumberledge, with whom Frank corresponded, took her place.

Frank's conversion to communism was not just a personal matter, but the result of world events, notably the Spanish Civil War, and of Frank's friends, the Carritts, who went to Spain to fight and die. I was almost equally affected by that war. I would not have fought but I would have driven an ambulance and probably got killed, like Julian Bell. But my father put his foot down, and persuaded me to continue my studies. I must be grateful. Frank always thought he was older than he was in reality; he was big. I always thought I was younger. I was small. Communism did seem to many intelligent people, such as Iris Murdoch, Maurice Dobb or Eric Hobsbawm, to be the answer to the iniquities of capitalism and imperialism.

Although perhaps, Conradi suggests, after Frank's death, Iris claimed too much for Frank's relationship with her, there can be no doubt about its importance for Frank. That is not to say that her declared love for MRD Foot drove Frank to suicidal exploits in Bulgaria. His support for the Bulgarian Resistance can be understood from his experience of the successful struggles of the Yugoslav Partisans in fighting the Nazis and from his determination that the Bulgarian resistance should be equally successful.

There was much distress for Frank's family in the long delay in the announcement of his death and in the unclear details of his capture and execution without trial or application of the Geneva Convention concerning captured enemy soldiers. But there does not seem, according to Conradi's review of the evidence, to be any justification for the wilder conclusions that Frank was deliberately abandoned by the British Army or as the result of any agreement to abandon him between the British and Soviet commands.

What this biography shows very clearly is Frank Thompson's warm hearted simplicity that any one who met him could recognise, and in his writing his belief in love and courage as his guiding principles. He had enormous admiration for the camaraderie, courage and resourcefulness of his fellow soldiers and not a moment's consciousness of class differences. To his two nearest and dearest, Iris Murdoch and his brother Edward, he begged them not to judge people by their class as others do, but to see them all as individuals. For someone in his early twenties this was remarkable wisdom. But he was truly much older than his age.

Frank's death at 23 was a tragic loss of a brilliantly talented and gifted young man. Just to record his linguistic ability, mastery of seven languages – English, Russian, Polish, German, Italian, French and Arabic – is to recognise an extraordinary person, and at the same time we have to notice his modesty and self-effacement. Every one complained of Frank's untidiness, but all had to accept his rejection of what he called 'psychological kit inspection'. In all things he followed his beloved Greeks in saying, 'Know thyself!'

Michael Barratt Brown

Ever Closer?

Jurgen Habermas, *The Crisis of the European Union: A Response*, Polity, 2012, 140 pages, hardback ISBN 9780745662428, £16.99

The old saw 'German jokes, they're no laughing matter!' can equally be true of German books, and Jurgen Habermas's *The Crisis of the European Union* is a perfect example. Here, one of Europe's pre-eminent philosophers is determined not to pander to those whose daily bread and butter is not moral philosophy and international law. A typical sentence is,

'The main challenge at the institutional level, however, is to recover the equal standing and symmetrical relation in the distribution of functions and legislative competences which we ascribe reconstructively to the European peoples and EU citizens as constitution-founding subjects' (p43).

It is somewhat of a relief that *The Crisis* is only 140 pages long. But more's the pity, because Habermas has some important things to say that peer out at intervals from the verbiage.

The book is an eclectic collection of Habermas's post-crisis writings; a long essay on the European Constitution, followed by the reprint of a paper on the concept of human dignity from the journal *Metaphilosophy*, an interview for *Die Zeit* on the European financial crisis, and two short articles for *Die Zeit* again and *Suddeutschen Zeitung*.

The paper on human dignity is the subordinate part of the book. In summary, Habermas pleads for it to become the core part of a reformed UN work, alongside global peacemaking. It is the idea of human dignity that underpins that of human rights, themselves a product of violent and, at times, revolutionary struggles. Presently, the highly selective and short-sighted decisions of a non-representative and far from impartial Security Council make for a suspicion that the programme of human rights consists of its imperialist misuse. That cannot be allowed to continue.

The core of the book is how to respond to the EU's ongoing travails. For Habermas the world financial crisis was a car crash just waiting to happen. Globalisation has so leapt ahead of political institutions that it has left nation states and coalitions of nation states completely incapable of exerting control over the global casino that purports to be the international financial institutions. The lunatics were left in control of the asylum. The job of politics is not to moralize but to act. The problem is that the European Union has been too slow, too cowardly and too conservative. Merkel dithered in the face of an imminent financial meltdown, and when she finally agreed to act – in concert with the other Eurozone leaders – she did the right thing in the wrong way. With her politics perhaps this is not really a surprise.

The proposals put into place a political steering mechanism to direct and drive European Economic and Monetary Union and promote competitiveness that will intrude far beyond fiscal policy into labour law and social policy that, in consequence, will rip out the heart of member state parliamentary purpose. Habermas does not cavil at this usurpation of sovereignty; rather he welcomes it as entirely necessary. For him, to not take such steps would be self-destructive and self-harming.

Whose hand will be on the tiller? The current proposals would institute an executive federalism that would set back democratic accountability by generations. There would be a loss of democracy at the European level that would de-legitimize its decisions. The answer is not 'less Europe', rather a demand and struggle for transnational democracy where individuals come to see themselves simultaneously as British and European, in which the European Parliament's powers match those of the Council of Ministers and the Commission becomes the executive arm of the two.

For Habermas the democratic process must be uncoupled from nation states, and there must be not only European Peoples but also European Citizens. If we are to escape the long shadow of nationalism, if we are to protect the European welfare state model, there is no alternative. To do this will not be easy.

Europe needs a constitutional debate to mirror that of September 1787 and August 1788 in North America. We need a Europeanisation of the existing party system. Social Democratic Parties must break out of their national cages and give themselves room to manoeuvre on the continental and global stage where our individual and collective future will play out.

It will be a David and Goliath fight. The asymmetry of interest and participation – partly media driven – in national and European politics tells its own story. But, if Habermas is right, the fight against climate change and for financial security, to control new technological threats and to maintain living standards can only be fought at a European level. He believes the failure of the European project is a real possibility. For those who want to know what that means, look to China. It disappeared from history for almost half a millennium. The danger in Britain – and European member states – is that national solipsism continues as the political orthodoxy.

Glyn Ford

Read widely

Philip Bounds, *British Communism and the Politics of Literature 1928-1939*, Merlin Press, 2012, 320 pages, paperback ISBN 9780850365948, 18.95

'The Communist Party of Great Britain was notorious for the low proportion of intellectuals in its ranks by comparison with the international communist movement as a whole.'
        John Gross, The Rise and Fall of the Man of Letters, *1969*

A sentence understandably not quoted by Bounds, who rebukes Gross for being 'deeply unfair' to most of the relevant ideologues, albeit happy to lean on him for details of J. C. Squire, seemingly unaware of Patrick Howarth's 1963 biography. While Gross cannot compare with the breadth, depth, and documentation of Bounds' widely acclaimed volume, his 20 pages win hands down for readability.

The veteran Bounds has read widely, albeit his homework is hard to mark, thanks to lack of formal Bibliography (partly redeemed by his annotated gallery of individuals and detailed Index), details having to be expiscated from 57 pages of end-notes, frequently mini-essays in themselves. The exposition is clear, laudably jargon-free, but stodgily prolix and repetitive, in urgent need of that now-extinct species, the sub-editor.

Claims to novelty are exaggerated. Apart from the complementary Neal Woods' *Communism and British Intellectuals* (1959; cf. Leon Epstein's review, *Political Science Quarterly* 75, 1960, 140-142), there is a 15-page essay at *sdonline.org*, also relevant treatments of CPGB history by, for example, Noreen Branson, James Eaden, and James Jupp – no 'astonishing neglect' here. Of adjacent interest, now, is Jamie Susskind's *Karl Marx and British Intellectuals in the 1930s* (2011).

Glances extra-Party would have illumined. Graham Greene's *It's a Battlefield* focuses communists and communism. Stalinists v. Trotskyists significantly preponderate in the 1930s narrative of Anthony Powell's *Dance to the Music of Time*.

Chapters One and Two (on 'Left Sectarianism' & 'Revolutionary Traditionalism') are a cornucopia of big names. One prominence is John Strachey, now best remembered for his groundnuts fiasco. Being a fellow-classicist, I was glad to see Australian-born Jack Lindsay here, albeit no mention of his *marxisant* novel *Rome for Sale*. There is also much on Eliot and Leavis from the other side.

Chapters Three to Five respectively focus on Alick West, Ralph Fox, and Christopher Caudwell. On this last, whose *Studies in a Dying Culture* remains alive and kicking, Bounds reluctantly acknowledges his inconsistencies, self-contradictions, and vapid rhetoric. I side with Gross' scornful dismissal of Caudwell in favour of Christopher Hill.

Chapter Six examines 'the wider *political* influences on British cultural Marxism', post-luded by a Conclusion largely devoted to Cultural Studies, a term generally credited to Richard Hoggart (1964) or (as Christopher Hitchens) to Raymond Williams. No mention of their guru, Stuart Hall's, classic 1989 lecture thereon. *Apropos* of Hall's 'encoding-decoding' nuances, fellow Brummie David Lodge makes his fictional Morris Zapp proclaim 'every decoding is another encoding'. I recall the wag who said 'Cultural Studies is just saying obvious things and pretending they mean something'.

This précis emphatically does not do justice to Bounds' bounds, richly extending from Aveling and Eleanor Marx to Gramsci and Raymond Williams. Still, as Palme Dutt (thrice mentioned) notoriously said of Stalin, there are spots on Bounds' sun. He reproduces the common misrepresentation of Edward Upward on Marxism as the only tenable literary basis. As Orwell (*Inside the Whale*) pointed out, Upward qualified this with his italicised '*at the present time*'. Talking of Orwell, it's unlikely (p. 243) that he filched material from Alec Brown, of whom he was so unaware as to muddle his name with Philip Henderson's (Peter Davison, *The Lost Orwell*, 2006, p. 170). C. L. R. James is oddly classified as 'non-communist'. Discreet anti-Trotskyism? No such qualification about T. A. Jackson, chiefly associated with the SPGB. Talking of Trotsky – unfairly denounced for 'self-dramatisation' – *Literature and Revolution* gets less than its due. MacLeish's *Frescoes* poem is not 'now forgotten', living widely on internet sites. Harold Heslop was no rarity as proletarian novelist; cf. the relevant online lists. And (a classicist's niggle), Caligula did not have his throat cut.

Select bibliographical addenda. Caudwell: Helena Sheehan, *Marxism and the Philosophy of Science* (1985), plus James Whetter, *A British Hero* (2011); Fox: *Ralph Fox: a Writer in Arms* (1937, ed. John Lehmann/T. A. Jackson/C. Day Lewis), also Eric Biddulph's online memoir; Alick West: one-time Trotskyist Peter Cadogan, *International Socialism* 3 (1960), 28 – online. Also, is the second Aveling-Marx lecture on *Shelley's Socialism* really lost (p. 34)? If so, all modern reprints deceive in advertising both.

Overall, Bounds overstates his case but there is a case to be overstated. Literary independence and political subservience must be distinguished. The latter can hardly be denied, e.g. in the cases of Palme Dutt, Harry Pollitt, the CPGB in 1939 and 1956 – look what happened to Peter Fryer's Hungarian reports. The 1930s intellectuals were hardly likely to display monolithic kow-towing to a 'Moscow line', given their own ideological and personal discords. Nor should a uniform Soviet cultural line be presumed. Here, Socialist Realism raises its controversial head. Bounds does not go into its origins enough, saying merely (p. 63) 'The term was allegedly coined by Stalin during a discussion with Maxim Gorki and others in 1932,' taking this (p. 266 n. 11) only from Cullerne Brown's *Art Under Stalin* (1991, p. 89), ignoring both Lynn Mally's 'Autonomous

Theatre and the Origins of Socialist Realism', *Russian Review* 52, 1993, 198-212, and the many articles and books of Herman Ermolaev, e.g. 'The Emergence and Early Evolution of Socialist Realism (1932-1934)', *California Slavic Studies* 2 (1963), 141-168. The term was first used in the 25 May 1932 issue of *Literaturnaya Gazeta*, the policy itself subsequently cooked up at the First Congress of Soviet Writers (1934). When announced by Ivan Gronsky, his literary audience jeered (Edward Radzinsky, *Stalin*, 1996, p. 271). Stalin himself (Mally, p. 207) was more concerned with creating an art 'socialist in content, national in form'. Later, though, Stalin caused consternation when, in 1950, his *Marxism and Problems of Linguistics* (rightly said by Robert Service, *Stalin*, 2004, p. 565, to be 'unjustly ignored') sensibly demolished Nicolai Marr's twaddle about bourgeois v. socialist Russian language by insisting that all languages were pre-capitalist in origin and (dialects apart) common to their speakers.

Despite aforementioned imperfections and some sense of *déjà lu*, this is a rich (my original 40 pages of notes and queries being their own tribute) synthetic/synoptic analysis of an important and ever-intriguing topic; a true display of haecceity. My appetite is whetted for his promised memoir of the Left in Wales – this Philip knows no bounds.

Barry Baldwin

Coalfield History

Jonathan Symcox (editor), *The 1984-1985 Miners' Strike in Nottinghamshire – The Diary of John Lowe*, Wharncliffe Books, 2011, paperback ISBN 9781845631444, £12.99

It is some 29 years since that epic struggle between the miners and the Conservative Government of Margaret Thatcher, and we can now clearly see it was a milestone victory for our indigenous élite in its drive towards intensifying inequality and restoring its paramount position in British society. This defeat, together with the continuing contrived levels of unemployment and anti-union legal enactments, has done much to critically weaken the trade unions. One of the clear messages to emerge from this contemporaneous diary is that the class war warriors of the Conservative Government were prepared to use all the forces of the state to crush the miners, whatever the financial cost.

This is the diary of one miner, an ordinary member of the NUM who, appalled by the inactivity of his local colliery officials as the strike escalated, took the initiative at his colliery, Clipstone, in organising a strike support committee for those workers prepared to heed the official strike call. By this action John Lowe proved, in the words of his grandson (a writer and journalist who edited this book) to be 'foremost a man of principle and honour'. As well as being a personal testimony and an important historical document, it is necessarily a very emotional record of commitment to a cause that split a community. The tone is well set in a moving foreword by Dennis Skinner, who knew the diarist growing up in Clay Cross.

A number of major themes flow through the diary, not least the level of officially sanctioned police violence and provocation, supported by a pliant media and endorsed by the local magistracy. Of the many incidents mentioned, two exemplify the harsh policing tactics. In one incident an infirm pensioner, over 70 years old, driving to see his daughter, was stopped at a police road-block. An ex-miner, he had the 'misfortune' to be wearing a 'coal not dole' badge on his lapel, and was dragged from his car, badly bruised, and his vehicle disabled by removal of the rotary arm. Collected by his son, the pair drove back to Mansfield, and were again stopped by police, and this time the son was dragged from the vehicle and both were taken to Mansfield police station. Then there is the whole episode of John Lowe's own arrest whilst on the picket line, which was both brutal and contrived by the police who consistently lied about a supposed assault. In the end John was fined and with costs had to pay £364.00 for, as he put it, 'sitting on the bloody grass'. The police, often with the compliance of some magistrates, were in many cases able to prevent bail and legal aid being granted, in order to increase hardship and increase the fear, and actuality, of being sent to Lincoln Prison. The use of undercover tactics, with people posing as sympathetic legal advisers or arrested miners (the latter being placed in cells with other arrested miners for the purpose of gathering information relating to a particular incident or the dispute in general) was common. Clearly, the police were under orders to provoke incidents where possible and to make life as difficult as they could for those picketing. One of the descriptions of police methods in the book compares them to wolves:

> 'When there's one he stands off and watches. When there's two they close in a little and still watch. When there's three they attack.'

The police are certainly one group of workers who prospered under the Thatcher dispensation, seeming to display the confident arrogance of assumed impunity, as the latest Hillsborough Inquiry has recently highlighted.

Things were financially tough for all the strikers from the outset of the dispute but, as the sequestration orders and the cumulative hardship intensified, it inevitably placed a great strain on their solidarity and cohesion. Matters were particularly difficult in the Nottinghamshire coalfield where, of course, the strikers were in a minority. Neighbours, friends and families were divided over the dispute, and public manifestations of conflict must have been relatively commonplace. The book records instances of many strikers receiving vitriolic anonymous letters and worse. The author only mentions sparingly, understandably so, the fact that he was at loggerheads with two of his sons over the dispute, which was very upsetting as he and his wife saw little of their grandchildren for a long period. The loss of contact with the children had a very serious effect on Elsie Lowe, John's wife, who supported him throughout the dispute and played an active role in the Women's Support Group.

The Women's Support Group was magnificent throughout the dispute, although they were no more immune to the ups-and-downs than the male Strike Committee, given the increasing hardship as the dispute persisted. The group played a major role in the successful struggle to obtain premises for a strike headquarters by the occupation of the Clipstone Welfare Youth Centre. During very hectic periods the Clipstone Women's Support Group was providing 300 meals a day. Their final act of defiance and support for the men was to turn out for the last picket when the delegate conference decided to end the dispute. The organising of the three daily picketing operations at the pit head, flying pickets around the county, managing the finances of the operation with insufficient funds, legal aid, fund raising, publicising and gathering support for the strikers – all this demonstrates the talents, intelligence and courage of working people faced with the might of the state.

The book has many photographs, some taken by John Lowe, but also facsimiles of letters, leaflets and documents which are both informative and evocative of the emotional temperature and locale of the dispute. Reading between the lines, the author must have had periods when he was doubtful of a successful outcome to the strike, although he remained outwardly optimistic throughout its duration despite the high personal cost. This was a battle that had to be fought, although the enemy had provoked conflict at a time when they were well prepared. However, he voices no substantial criticism of the union leadership, except to say that they did not take into account sufficiently the minority position of the Nottinghamshire strikers and the threat of the NUM locally to break away from the union. He does have harsh words for the Kinnock leadership, the local Labour MP at the time, Don Concannon, and other trade union leaders who failed to show sufficient real support for the miners. As for the scabs' union, the Union of Democratic Mineworkers, only recently it recorded another chapter in its ignominious decomposition with one of its former leaders, Neil Greatrex, convicted of the theft of £150,000 from a miners' nursing and residential home. The union had previously been criticised for paying its top officials 'fat cat' levels of remuneration, and the Labour MP for Bassetlaw, John Mann, has called on the police to renew their investigation into the UDM's connection with solicitors who were struck off for overcharging and inadequate attention to miners' injury compensation claims (*The Guardian*, 03/04/2012).

This is an inspiring book that deserves to be read widely, particularly in the Nottinghamshire area, which has never really recovered economically from the destruction of the coal industry. Whilst the full story of the strike and its aftermath in the Nottinghamshire Coalfield, including the final closures by the Major government, has yet to be told, this book will be an invaluable source and guide. The diary also stands as a fitting memorial to a true working class hero, John Lowe, who died in 2005.

John Daniels

Occupy!

Michael Albert, Mark Evans, Mandini Majavu, David Marty and Jessica Azulay, *Fanfare for the Future Vol. 1: Occupy Theory, Vol. 2: Occupy Vision and Vol. 3: Occupy Strategy*, Z Books, 2012, Kindle Editions (ISBNs – none available)

Toward the end of 2011, the global Occupy! movement began to capture the imaginations of all those in society who hankered after change. The people, the 99% as they came to be known, were calling for a change to the way the social order was constructed and managed. This call to transform society from a corporate-led machine to something in which we can all participate is still being advanced today.

The peaceful mass sit-ins of Occupy!, coupled with the sometimes violent revolutions in the Middle East and North Africa, not too mention the protests in Portugal, Spain and Greece, highlight a rejection of the existing system by many citizens. Revolutions and protests are, by their very nature, ways of changing how society functions.

It is this alteration to the way the world works that is at the heart of the three volumes in the *Fanfare for the Future* series. As the authors say,

> 'Fanfare for the Future is three volumes about winning social changes that reorient whole societies by altering institutions at the heart of the lives of all people'.

The transformation of the system comes from the people who face difficulties on a day-to-day basis, and these three books are aimed directly at them.

The three volumes are written with the purpose of enabling readers to think for themselves about the best ways to alter society. In order to achieve this, the authors suggest that we need to think differently about the world around us. To help readers understand how to change things, the authors propose that we get to grips with where to start, what the final goal is, and what's the best way of getting from A to B.

Occupy Theory (Vol. 1) presents issues highlighted by the movement, such as greed and corruption, and asks readers to consider the best ways in which to address such problems. The authors identify four structures of society that have most impact upon people's lives: the economy, kinship, culture and polity. These structures, they argue, enable society to function, but if one of them fails to function efficiently, then something must be done to fix it. Many social problems are caused by a malfunction in one (or more) of these four areas, and the authors cite the economic crisis of 2007-2008, wars, poverty and unemployment as prime examples of such failures.

Occupy Vision (Vol. 2) presents a case for what the future could look like based on the ideas in Volume 1. It builds on what needs changing, as discussed in *Occupy Theory*, by offering alternative ways for society to be structured:

> 'The result is not capitalist, not 20th century socialist, not authoritarian, not sexist or heterosexist, not racist or nationalistic, not ecocidal, and not imperialist. It is, instead, in its values and its institutions: participatory economic, self-managing, feminist, intercommunalist, peaceful.'

The final volume, *Occupy Strategy*, addresses the approach and tactics required to bring about a participatory society that would realise the vision set out in *Occupy Vision*.

All three titles are easy to read and understand, and they pay due homage to the Occupy! movement of 2011/12. In both the movement and the *Fanfare* series, to 'occupy' means to take a space used for one purpose and use it for something else. The space within these books is used to present ideas about how to change society, which can then be 're-purposed' by those who are disenfranchised. They provide a small platform from which readers can begin to connect ideas and make a difference to our world.

Abi Rhodes

Corporate Paranoia

Evelin Lubbers, *Secret Manoeuvres in the Dark – Corporate and Police Spying on Activists*, Pluto Press, 2012, 272 pages, hardback ISBN 9780745331867, £66.50, paperback ISBN 9780745331850, £19.99

Was this book originally a doctoral thesis? It's a pretty dull read. As all doctoral dissertations have to be, it is well researched – almost over-researched. The references get in the way of a smooth read. While you are happily reading along, there is (see Barratt Brown 5000 BC, Coates 1850, Potter 1940, Simpson 2011). See what I mean? All this reference tends to get in the way. Has the author never heard of footnotes? It is an earnest, worthy, over-intense work that could have been better farmed out as a monograph, or a long essay in the *London Review of Books*. Too long, alas, for *The Spokesman*!

If the author wants a wider public, she will be doomed to disappointment. A pity, because the message is an important one: big business will go to almost any lengths to cripple its critics; lying, spying and infiltrating are the names of the games. Have you, dear reader, ever participated in any kind of completely legal form of dissent? CND? Moves against Monsanto? MacDonalds? Shell? The weapons trade? And many more who put profit before all else. You will, probably, have been spied on, lied to and betrayed.

Let us take an imaginary example that represents many of the cases that appear in the book: I strike up a correspondence with Ken Coates and Tony Simpson. They don't give much away, but when they ask me to write a review, they let slip they will be publishing an article about a certain person or organisation. *The Spokesman* being a Lefty magazine, the article will almost certainly be critical. I pass the news on so that those criticised are ready with the PR and spin to rubbish *The Spokesman*. You get the idea. Don't trust anyone. Paranoia, if it exists at all, is a rare condition. They usually *are* out to get you, spy on you, lie to you, betray you, and destroy or dismantle and disarm you.

The author, in her boring, pedantic way, warns us that all this secrecy, these hidden agendas are a threat to 'Democracy'. Now, I wonder, which democracies did she have in mind? Most of the democracies I know are one-party states and, of course, have their élites. The oligarchs will take almost any measures to protect their interests and push their business and profits. So what else is new?

Actually, *Secret Manoeuvres in the Dark* is quite reassuring. Liberals who plough their way through this academic stuff will raise their hands in horror. 'It didn't ought to be allowed. Something must be done!' But they should be calmed. Democracy is at work. It is extraordinary that big business goes to such extraordinary lengths, and at such cost, to deflate its opponents. In many parts of the world they wouldn't bother. They would just whack 'em.

Nigel Potter
Honduras

Peacock and bird carpet c. 1800s.
Displayed at 'Pre Raphaelites: Victoria Avant-Garde',
Tate Britain (see page 55).